120
148
fight
teraction
merica
150, 154
146

Against Fairness

STEPHEN T. ASMA

Against
Fairness

The University of Chicago Press

Chicago and London

STEPHEN T. ASMA is a distinguished scholar and professor of philosophy in the Department of Humanities, as well as a fellow of the Research Group in Mind, Science, and Culture at Columbia College Chicago. He is the author of several books, including *On Monsters, Stuffed Animals and Pickled Heads,* and *Following Form and Function.*

The University of Chicago Press, Chicago 60637
The University of Chicago Press, Ltd., London
© 2013 by Stephen T. Asma
All rights reserved. Published 2013.
Printed in the United States of America

22 21 20 19 18 17 16 15 14 13   1 2 3 4 5

ISBN-13: 978-0-226-02986-3 (cloth)
ISBN-10: 0-226-02986-7 (cloth)
ISBN-13: 978-0-226-92346-8 (e-book)
ISBN-10: 0-226-92346-0 (e-book)

Library of Congress Cataloging-in-Publication Data

Asma, Stephen T.
    Against fairness / Stephen T. Asma.
      pages; cm
    Includes bibliographical references and index.
    ISBN 978-0-226-02986-3 (cloth: alkaline paper) — ISBN 0-226-02986-7 (cloth: alkaline paper) — ISBN 978-0-226-92346-8 (e-book) — ISBN 0-226-92346-0 (e-book) 1. Fairness. 2. Preferences (Philosophy) 3. Values. 4. Nepotism. I. Title.
    BJ1533.F2A86 2012
    179—dc23   2012013887

⊚ This paper meets the requirements of ANSI/NISO Z39.48-1992 (Permanence of Paper).

For my favorite.

He knows who he is.

CONTENTS

ACKNOWLEDGMENTS

As with all my books, I owe a debt of gratitude to my supportive family. My tribe is a wonderfully diverse clan of generous and caring kin. Many thanks to Wen Rong Jin, beloved lioness of our little family. Thanks to my parents, Ed and Carol; my brothers, Dave and Dan; and the whole Asma clan: Keaton, Maddy, Garrison, Elaine.

As Aristotle said: Without friends, no one would choose to live. Special thanks goes to my excellent partners of the Research Group in Mind, Science, and Culture: Tom Greif, Rami Gabriel, and Glenn Curran. Our many readings and discussions indirectly helped to shape this book. And the friendship is absolutely invaluable.

I am grateful to friends and supporters across several institutions: Cheryl Johnson-Odim, Deborah Holdstein, the incomparable Jaak Panksepp, Louise Love, Micki Leventhal, Brent White, Zahava Doering. And a special tip of the hat to my friends Baheej and Susan, Peter Altenberg, Jim Christopulos, and Brian Wingert.

Others need to be thanked: Alex Kafka, Raja Halwani, Lynn and Allen Turner, Dave Eddington, Tomo, Elif, and my other friends at the Lake Shore Unitarian Society, Michael Shermer, Donna Seaman, Alison Cuddy, Carrie Shepherd, Aurora Aguilar, Adrienne Mayor, Michael Sims, Giles Anderson, Shifu Paula Lazarz, Joanna Ebenstein, and the great musicians (Rami Gabriel and Bryan Pardo) of my band, Swing Hakim.

Many thanks to my wonderful editor at University of Chicago Press, Elizabeth Branch Dyson, who believed in this controversial project and gave it the care and attention it needed. Thanks also to her assistant, Russell Damian, promotions manager Ryo Yamaguchi, and copy editor Erin DeWitt. I am also very grateful to Barry Schwartz for reading the manuscript and offering insightful advice. Of course, the remaining flaws in the book are all mine.

Finally, I acknowledge my greatest devotion: my favorite, my son, my Julien.

1

Even Jesus Had a Favorite

"I would strangle everyone in this room if it somehow prolonged my son's life." That's what I blurted into a microphone during a panel discussion on ethics. I was laughing when I said it, but the priest sitting next to me turned sharply in horror and the communist sitting next to him raised her hand to her throat and stared daggers at me. Why was I on a panel with a priest and a revolutionary communist? Long story—not very interesting: we were debating the future of ethics with special attention to the role of religion. The interesting part, however, is that at some point, after we all shook hands like adults and I was on my way home, I realized that I meant it—I would choke them all. Well, of course, one can't be entirely sure that one's *actions* will follow one's intentions. The best-laid plans of mice and men, and all that. But, given some weird *Twilight Zone* scenario wherein all their deaths somehow saved my son's life, I was at least hypothetically committed. The caveman intentions were definitely there.

If some science-fiction sorcerer came to me with a button and said that I could save my son's life by pressing it, but then (cue the dissonant music) ten strangers would die somewhere . . . I'd have my finger down on it before he finished his cryptic challenge. If he raised it to one hundred strangers, a million, or the whole population, it would still take the same microsecond for me to push the button.

The utilitarian demand—that I should always maximize the greatest good for the greatest number—seemed reasonable to me in my twenties but made me laugh after my son was born. My draconian bias is not just the testosterone-fueled excesses of the male psyche. Mothers can be aggressive lionesses when it comes to their offspring. Mothers are frequently held up as the icons of selfless nurturing love, but that's because we offspring—the ones holding them up as icons— are the lucky recipients of that biased love. From *that* point of view, a mother's behavior is infinitely charitable. But if you're outside the clan, then tread carefully. Try getting between a mammal mother and her kid, and you will see natural bias at its brutal finest.

So, as I learned, becoming a parent brings some new emotional "organs" with it, some organs I never would have thought possible to grow in me just five years earlier. These "organs" process the intense protective biases—the "chemicals"—of family solidarity. How do we square these preferential emotions with our larger social ethics?

Americans are taught, from an early age, that no one is intrinsically "higher" or "lower" than anyone else, that everyone is equally valuable. Philosopher Martha Nussbaum says, "Our nation is built on the idea that all citizens as citizens are of equal worth and dignity."[1] So how do we reconcile our favoritism with our conflicting sense of equality for all?

Some theorists explain this inner conflict as a fight between our raw animal emotions and our rational (principled) system of the good (impartial justice). But that makes things easy—too easy. The tension between preference and fairness is not just between the individual heart and the collective head. Rather it is a tension between two competing notions of the good.

Charles Darwin argued that the moral life itself is actually built upon the tribal devotions of our ancestors. The foundation of morality lies in the social instincts, including under this term the family ties. These instincts are highly complex, and in the case of the lower animals give special tendencies toward certain definite actions; but the more important elements are love, and the distinct emotion of sympathy. Animals endowed with the social instincts take pleasure in one another's company, warn one another of danger, defend and aid one another in many ways. These instincts do not extend to all the individuals of the species, but only those of the same community.[2]

And it is perhaps this last line, about the provincialism of our instinctual devotions, that will most concern us in this book about favoritism. Is it really primitive, as the egalitarians claim, to privilege some over others?

Saints and Favorites

It's hard to imagine someone more fair-minded and even self-sacrificing than Jesus. The list of his ethical peers is short: maybe Buddha, Gandhi, Mother Teresa, Martin Luther King, some miscellaneous saints and martyrs. Fill in the blanks. Jesus was such an equal-opportunity humanitarian that he regularly went to eat and spend time with the outcasts, the prostitutes, the tax collectors, and the pariahs. He liked just about everybody and encouraged us to do the same. He took his goodwill one step further, of course, and recommended that we should even love our enemies. This indiscriminate love is arguably the central teaching of Christianity.

And yet, even Jesus, the paragon of equal treatment, had a *favorite* disciple. We don't know for sure which disciple it was—most think it was John—but we're told in the Gospels that he had a favorite one, and that he even had a three-man inner circle. He had a posse *inside* his posse.

Another holy man that earns our respect for his selfless charity and his leveling egalitarian approach is Siddhattha Gotama, the Buddha. He pushed the bounds of fairness through all the caste-system boundaries of Indian society and arrived at a totally impartial social and even

Fig. 1. Jesus calling some of his favorites (John and James) to follow him.
Drawing by Stephen Asma, based on a Byzantine painting.

metaphysical philosophy. Not only could women and untouchables attain enlightenment—a scandalous idea at the time—but every animal species was put on equal status too. And yet, despite all this philosophical impartiality, the Buddha had a best friend, Ananda, who had no equal among the Buddha's associates. The Enlightened One had a right-hand man.

Is it *fair* for me to pit the universal egalitarianism of many religions against the favoritism of family and friends? Surely one need not preclude the other. In some passages of the New Testament, for example, the tension is not between filial love and universal love, but between filial love and Jesus devotion. "For I am come to set a man at variance against his father, and the daughter against her mother, and the daughter-in-law against her mother-in-law. And a man's foes shall be they of his own household. He that loveth father or mother more than me is not worthy of me: and he that loveth son or daughter more than me is not worthy of me" (Matthew 10:35–37). This suggests a contest of allegiance, pitting one set of favorites for a new one. Philosopher Bertrand Russell was not a fan. "All this means the breakup of the biological family tie for the sake of creed—an attitude which had a great deal to do with the intolerance that came into the world with the spread of Christianity."[3] But one of the great Eastern saints of the twentieth century, Gandhi, also recognized the incompatibility between spiritualism and favoritism.

In his autobiography, Gandhi suggested that saintliness required forfeiture of the usual bonds of family and friendship. The seeker of goodness, Gandhi recommended, must have no close friendships or

Fig. 2. Gandhi (1869–1948) argued that we must abandon our "favorites" if we are to love everyone. Drawing by Stephen Asma.

exclusive loves because these will introduce loyalty, partiality, bias, and favoritism. In order to love *everyone*, we must not preferentially love any individual or group.

When George Orwell read Gandhi's autobiography in 1948, he was deeply troubled by the Indian saint's "anti-humanism." It's hard for us to envision Gandhi—lover of all mankind—as anti-humanist. But Orwell viewed any attempt to subjugate human values to the demands of some transcendent, ideological value system as anti-human. While Orwell remained impressed by Gandhi's political achievements, he was stunned by Gandhi's views on friendship and family. Saintly egalitarianism seemed repugnant to Orwell, who believed that "love means nothing if it does not mean loving some people more than others."[4]

I want to side definitively with Orwell here and cannot follow the Indian saint to his lofty conclusion. I must agree with Orwell's claim that "the essence of being human is that one does not seek perfection, that one is sometimes willing to commit sins for the sake of loyalty . . . and that one is prepared in the end to be defeated and broken up by life, which is the inevitable price of fastening one's love upon other human individuals."[5]

Gandhi's saintly ideal of *non-attachment* may not be compatible with the humanistic ideal, which maintains that this flawed world (with all its liabilities of attachment) is the only one we have. But in a way, the ideal of non-attachment is also secretly at work in some of our more dogmatic liberal traditions of universal equality for all.

Gandhi is perhaps an outlier, an extremist against favoritism. But his radical position helps us grasp the philosophical tensions between fairness and favoritism. Buddha, with his bff Ananda, was not as extreme in his detachment. And one suspects that Gandhi, despite his own advice, wasn't either. In fact, Gandhi's relationship with Jewish architect Hermann Kallenbach, whom he met in South Africa, looks extremely intimate and seems to violate every one of the guru's ideals of detachment.[6]

I'm not a particularly religious person. I'm not overly impressed by Buddhas, Mahatmas, or Messiahs. I'm actually a skeptical agnostic most days, but I start with these religious "exemplars of equality" for dramatic effect. Why do even these major saints of universal love and impartiality still have favorites? Why do they discriminate at all, if everybody is equally valuable? The answer, I will argue in this book, is that they can't do otherwise. It is human to prefer. Love is discriminatory. And if the world's scriptures can be believed, even the gods have preferences. The monotheistic God is no better on this account than the polytheistic traditions. The Abrahamic God often gets jealous, has "chosen people," and generally plays favorites.

None of this is breaking news, of course. So what's new in my approach to the favoritism/fairness divide? While everyone has a general sense that favoritism feels natural and that fairness vies against it, philosophers and leaders have almost always sided *with* fairness and *against* favoritism. Religious leaders have agreed that we *tend* toward preference and bias, but we should generally resist this pull and fight our own inner discriminatory tendencies. Biologists and social theorists, since Darwin, have joined the ranks of anti-bias, by arguing that our animal nature might be selfish, but our uniquely human capacities allow us to fight against our animal natures.[7] Implicit in this idea, that our better angels can subdue our baser instincts, is the assumption that these instincts are selfish—are focused on *self*-preservation.[8] But this assumption has skewed the conversation into a false dichotomy: either you're for yourself, or you're for fairness. A recent example of this false dichotomy can be found in Peter Corning's otherwise insightful book *The Fair Society*, in which he assumes that opposition to fairness is tantamount to Ayn Rand–style individual selfishness.[9] I share Corning's and other sane people's aversion to the Ayn Rand cult of self-interest (an ethic endorsed by Alan Greenspan). But I don't agree that the solution or forced alternative is egalitarian fairness.

I want to argue that a huge part of our values has been left out of this usual dichotomy, namely, our *tribal* biases. Our values landscape is not a hill of fairness and a valley of selfishness. The bonds of our affections (our biases) are not reducible to either selfishness or selflessness, but require their own autonomous territory. Family ties, for example, don't fit neatly into the usual dichotomy of selfish/selfless values. Bias, nepotism, and tribal ethics have taken it on the chin for too long. Against an army of pious guides and gurus, I will try to make the case for favoritism.

When I explained to my friends that I was writing a book called *Against Fairness*, they looked at me like I had made some final descent into madness. I might as well write a book *Against Mothers* or *Against Oxygen*. On the face of it, the project looks insane. But I don't mind an uphill battle. Let me begin, then, by offering some provisional definitions of terms like "tribal," "fairness," and "nepotism."

Fairness, Tribes, and Nephews

"Tribal" may be a confusing term. For many readers, the term will have inescapable connotations of Africa or an indigenous ethnic clan from some exotic region. There's nothing wrong with this. Tribal can indeed describe the Zulus of southern Africa or the Apache of the American Southwest. But I wish to use the broader meaning of tribal, such that it also describes an extended family, a nuclear family, and possibly even your bowling team. A tribe, in this informal sense, is a social group of members who have greater loyalty to one another than to those *outside* the group. A tribe is an *us* in a milieu of *thems*. And the defining properties of each tribe might differ significantly—it could be blood that ties a tribe together; it could be class, language, race, or a mutual devotion to *Doctor Who* or *The Big Lebowski*.

Twentieth-century anthropology searched for a *logic* of tribes. Many researchers believed that some common formal essence or structural grid underlay the various tribes. They searched for a similar recipe of ingredients in every cultural case. Every time they settled on some precise definition, they'd come upon tribes that didn't fit the bill. In response to this, more recent researchers have given up the search for a structural *essence* and accepted the amoeba-like malleability of tribes. Tribes are highly flexible, and they adapt to local challenges.[10]

It is also insufficient to think of tribes in purely evolutionary terms. We often find analysts, especially in the "clash of civilizations" debate, talking about tribes as a step or stage—one that's on its way to becoming a state. There might be some other argument for claiming that tribes are primitive, but there seems to be little evidence that tribes are always supplanted or replaced by later kinds of political organization. Even when many different groups coalesce, by choice or force,

low
LARGE
+ u
T TRIBE ?

tribal affiliations can continue within larger organizations of power and authority. Clans and cliques don't always go extinct when states evolve into existence.

Most important, perhaps, is this: The fact that there have been some very nasty and hostile tribes throughout history does not nullify the tribe as a valid form of social organization. I cannot underscore this point enough. Just because there are some bad motorcycle gangs or bankers or skateboarders, for example, does not mean that these groups are *intrinsically* deviant or corrupt. And yet a similarly sloppy logic has animated many objections to tribes, clans, cliques, and factions. We will need to begin our inquiry, at least, without assuming a contemptuous view of tribes.

What do we mean by "fairness"? Etymologically, the term "fair" seems to have originated as an aesthetic term, describing someone beautiful or pleasant. Only gradually did the term migrate to the ethical domain, where it tended to mean a person or action that was unblemished by moral stain. When something is fair, it is generally considered free from bias and prejudice. If it's used as an adjective for social interaction or for a distribution of goods, then it generally implies an *equal* measure for concerned parties. Philosopher John Rawls took fairness to be the key ingredient in justice, stating that "fundamental to justice, is the concept of fairness which relates to right dealing between persons who are cooperating with or competing against each other, as when one speaks of fair games, fair competition, and fair bargains."[11] And somewhere in the background of our usual thinking about fairness is the assumption of the equality of all mankind—egalitarianism.[12]

The idea of universal respect is endorsed in both the modern secular and the ancient sacred traditions of the West. Our biblical traditions sometimes assert that human equality can be found in the idea that we were all made in God's image, and our government documents affirm equality on the grounds of inalienable rights that were endowed by our Creator.[13] Philosophers generally agree that modern Western society is premised on egalitarian ideology. We've already seen philosopher Martha Nussbaum's claim that all citizens are of equal worth. And philosopher Charles Taylor reminds us that "the average person needs to do very little thinking about the bases of universal respect . . . because just about everyone accepts this as an axiom today." Moreover, Taylor suggests that tribal thinking is uncivilized because it draws its circles of respect narrowly, while "higher civilizations" include the whole human species in their circle of respect.[14]

Generally speaking, our ideologies run in favor of fairness and equal treatment. Some of us might even assume that we are always upholding this principle. Ironically, some Westerners even assume that it is their commitment to equality and fairness that makes them *superior* to other individuals and cultures. It is our notion of equality that makes us the "higher" tribe.

In this ironic formulation, we can smell a burning friction between two concepts. The concept that everybody gets an *equal share* of the good scrapes up against another concept of fairness: winner takes all, or at least takes more. When merit or skill trumps the competitor, we generally think it is fair to apportion more reward. May the best man win, as we say. Merit deserves more. But this merit-based fairness vies against "equal shares" or "equal outcomes" fairness.

Jesus trades on these competing concepts in his paradoxical parable of the workers in the vineyard (Matthew 20:1–16). A householder farmer goes out in the morning and hires some workers to labor in his vineyard, promising them one silver denarius for a full day's work. At midday the farmer hires another crew to join the vineyard work, and in the final hour of the workday he hires yet another team. When all the laborers finish at nightfall, they return and the farmer pays them all the exact same wage—one silver denarius each. Adding insult to injury, the farmer rebukes the all-day workers who complain about the inequity.

I remember hearing this parable in church when I was a kid and feeling bad for the suckers who had sweated all day for the same wage as the eleventh-hour laborers. I was soothed by priests, who explained that God saves by grace, not by merit. I was told that deeds—no matter how rigorous or pious—cannot really earn God's rewards. Just *ask* and you can receive the kingdom of heaven. No one actually *deserves* salvation, and God will bestow it on sinners and saints equally *if* their hearts are sufficiently contrite. This may indeed be the true lesson of the parable, but for our purposes the story also illustrates the tension between fairness as equal outcomes and fairness as merit system.

Our contemporary hunger for equality can border on the comical. When my six-year-old son came home from first grade with a fancy winner's ribbon, I was filled with pride to discover that he had won a footrace. While I was heaping praise on him, he interrupted to correct me. "No, it wasn't just me," he explained. "We *all* won the race!" He impatiently educated me. He wasn't first or second or third—he couldn't even remember what place he took. Everyone who ran the race was told that they had *won*, and they were all given the same ribbon. "Well, you can't *all* win a race," I explained to him, ever-supportive father that I am. That doesn't even make sense. He simply held up his purple ribbon and raised his eyebrows at me, as if to say, "You are thus refuted."

Shortly after this comedy, he informed me of another curious school district policy—one that's been around the United States for a few decades. It's trivial perhaps, but telling. If my son wanted to bring some Valentine's Day cards for his classmates, we were told that he would have to bring one for *every* member of his class. No favoritism was to be tolerated. No one's fragile self-esteem would be put to that awful test. The school legislates that all valentine outcomes will be equal.

In a similar case, school drama and music teachers complain these days that it is extremely difficult to put on plays, because they must try to find productions and scripts that contain equal numbers of lines for each student. Some parents will count the number of lines for each part and raise hell if their child is upstaged by another student.[15]

More troubling than the institutional enforcement of this strange fairness is the fact that such protective "lessons" ill-equip kids for the realities of later life. As our children grow up, they will have to negotiate a world of partiality. Does it really help children when our schools legislate reality into a "fairer" but utterly fictional form? The focus on equality of *outcome* may produce a generation that is burdened with an indignant sense of entitlement.

But our cultural appetite for excellence in sports and arts shows that merit-based concepts of fairness are also very strong. When peo-

ple feel self-conscious about the "socialist" implications of their belief
in equal shares, they will often try to purify their convictions about
fairness by switching to the meritocracy version. Okay, they say, it's
actually more fair to give people what they really deserve (by excellence of skill or talent).

The beloved children's folktale *The Little Red Hen* embodies some
of this merit-based fairness. Recall that the red hen works very hard
planting and tending wheat, then harvesting, grinding, and baking it.
All the while, she is pleading with her friends to help her, but they are
too lazy and refuse. Finally, when the wheat is baked into delicious
bread, the friends want to help her eat the bread, but she serves them
a cold plate of fairness by eating all the bread herself.

At first, readers may think that I'm making an all-too-familiar refinement or purification of fairness. Oh, you might think, he's just
playing a conservative card of entrepreneurial gumption against lazy
social welfare handouts. But actually I will be arguing something
much more controversial: The rewards of favoritism do not need to
follow the accomplishments of merit or even excellence. Favoritism
flies in the face of *both* concepts of fairness—meritocracy and equal
share distribution.

Another term, "nepotism," will be important throughout this book.
What is nepotism? Favoritism is not just a belief or set of feelings. I
might have stronger feelings for members of my tribe, but the ethical
issues that really interest us are matters of *action*. How do I *act* on my
favoritism? What are the *behaviors* that stem from favoritism?

I will use the term "nepotism" to describe the values and actions of
favoritism. "Nepotism" has become a dirty word—most people use it
synonymously with "corruption." But the word is a Latin term, *nepos*,
that really means "nephew," "grandchild," or "descendant." Nepotism
is behavior that privileges your family.[16] I will use it in its expanded
sense—behavior that privileges your tribe.

It is common for Westerners to sanction nepotism in private life
but denounce it in public life. Never mind the hopeless task of drawing a clear line between private and public, let's simply recognize that
I can help my brother get a job at the factory where I work, but if I'm a

congressman, then I might be charged with malfeasance for a similar act of nepotism. We have an official culture that formally rejects personal ties and preferential treatment.

This is not as universal as we think, though. Things are quite different in the East. Having lived for a while in China and Cambodia, I can confirm some of the stereotypes of Asian nepotism—but of course unlike most commentators, I'm a fan of this stuff, not a foe. Asia and the Middle East are "face cultures" in the sense that social or public regard is absolutely crucial for success. And *who* you know is paramount. This is not just recognized privately (as it is in the West), but also officially.

In Chinese culture (which is more communal than American individualism), you need to build elaborate connections with friends, coworkers, and neighbors. *Guanxi* is the Chinese word for "good connections," and without *guanxi* you're going nowhere fast. Being useful to people is perhaps the best way to build up *guanxi*, but also "giving face" or respect (in Chinese: *gei mianzi*) to elders, superiors, or friends can build up strong ties for when you eventually need help yourself.

Getting our son into a good preschool in China, for example, was an elaborate ritual in which we had to find friends of friends and relatives of relatives who could "connect" in some remote way (by blood or acquaintance) to a staff member in the school's administration office. Then we had to have a sit-down with everyone present—no e-mails or phone calls for serious business in a "face culture." You must sit down and drink tea, face-to-face. You don't fill out an application for things and trust that bureaucracy will give you your opening. You grease wheels. You curry favor.

Nepotism is not just *tolerated* in many other cultures; it is in fact the coin of the realm. What people object to is not nepotism per se but the *abuse* of nepotism. This is hard to understand if you were raised in an official culture where every case of nepotism is seen as an abuse. In many face cultures, however, nepotism is a matter of *degree*, and it only becomes corruption when it scales up to obnoxious excess. Middle East scholar Lawrence Rosen relates a funny story of a conversation with Berber friends in a Moroccan home. As they were eating their main meal after prayers on a Friday afternoon, Rosen's friend Hussein asked him if there was corruption in the United States. At first Rosen suggested Watergate as an example, but Hussein and the others dismissed this as just *siyasa*, politics. When Rosen offered an example of nepotism, his Moroccan friends replied, "No, no, no . . . that is just *'a'ila*, family solidarity."[17] When Rosen, slightly exasperated, pressed his friends to define corruption, they described it as a failure to share with one's companions and allies. "Corruption is, in the Arabic idiom, 'to eat' the good things that should be shared with others."[18]

It is not only the Eastern examples that give us some perspective on our Western ways. Our own history gives us insight into how far the contemporary view has changed. When the seventeenth-century Pope Urban VIII lay on his deathbed, he summoned a group of church canonists to examine his nepotism track record.[19] He wanted to enter the pearly gates with a clear conscience, so he submitted a list of all the gifts that he had bestowed on his *nepotes*, nephews. Had he exceeded the bounds of family generosity? Of course, the private commission exonerated him and assured him of easy passage to the great beyond. But what's interesting about this case is not whether they were right—subsequent biographers found Urban VIII to be overly lavish in his gift giving. What is interesting is that no one viewed nepotism itself as corruption. It was assumed by all that wealth (especially sudden good fortune, as was the case for Urban) should be preferentially dispensed to family first. Those outside your tribe should also reap some surplus benefits, of course. The goods, whatever they may be, should radiate out in concentric circles from the fortunate benefactor. Favoritism was not a sin—quite the contrary, sensible nepotism was actually considered virtuous. Immoderate or intemperate indulgence of one's favorites was the problem.[20]

Two Classic Cases of Favoritism

In order to make my case for favoritism, I have to leave the arid realm of abstract generalizations and focus on specific cases. The details really matter, because our unique bonds of affection tie to distinct personalities. So I want to introduce two important cases—from Confucius and

Socrates—that will also serve as helpful touchstones throughout later sections of the book.

A Chinese politician from an outlying province attempted to impress Kongzi (Confucius) with an anecdote of local virtue. The politician explained that the people of his region were so morally upright that if a father steals a sheep, the son will give evidence against him. While the politician was basking in the righteousness of his story, Kongzi replied, "Our people's uprightness is not like that. The father shields his son, the son shields his father. There is uprightness in this."[21]

No more is said about this exchange in Kongzi's famous *Analects*, and no unified interpretation can be found in two millennia of Confucian philosophy. But, of course, most of us know exactly what Kongzi meant. We know it in our bones, even if we can't articulate it in language.

It is difficult to express an idea of moral privilege when almost all of our ethical education has been against it. From children's stories to religious parables to technical philosophies, we are encouraged to eliminate our personal connections from considerations of justice. The idea of fairness that many of us are raised on requires us to assign all parties equal weight. Lady Justice herself is often represented as blindfolded when she balances her scales. She cannot factor in people's money, status, or power, and she cannot play favorites. But I would side with Kongzi's ethic rather than the impartial politician's.

When philosopher Bertrand Russell read this Confucian passage, he took it as both refreshingly honest and indicative of a large-scale difference in Eastern and Western ethics. Russell generally thought that Christian virtue was too extreme—demanding charity for everyone, including one's enemies. Confucian ethics, on the other hand, is more moderate and therefore more attainable. Instead of loving one's enemies and treating everyone as equals, the Chinese person, according to Russell, is expected "to be respectful to his parents, kind to his children, generous to his poor relations, and courteous to all. These are not very difficult duties," Russell observes, "but most men actually fulfill them, and the result is perhaps better than that of our higher standard, from which most people fall short."[22] The Confucian ethic,

Fig. 3. Lady Justice, the allegorical personification of impartial fairness.
In ancient depictions she is not blindfolded, but modern representations emphasize
the need to eradicate subjective bias. Drawing by Stephen Asma.

which embraces favoritism, is less susceptible to the familiar Western hypocrisy—the pretense of believing we can be saints, but all the
while acting like mere mortals.

Kongzi would not have been a fan of Jesus' universal love, which
tries to turn the other cheek for slapping abuses and worse. Kongzi
knew about more universal notions of love, from his Daoist contemporaries, but it seemed incoherent to him. Daoist philosophers of the
day regularly promoted the idea that one should return good for evil.
But when asked about this pious policy, Kongzi replied, "What then is
to be the return for good?"[23]

For Confucian thinkers, integrity is not synonymous with fairness
or equality. Rather, familial love and devotion trump all other duties
and obligations. There is a natural hierarchy of values, with one's kin

on top, and Confucian culture enshrines, rather than denies, that hierarchy.

Many of us have been raised to think that favoritism is inconsistent with morality and justice. Enlightenment philosophers like Immanuel Kant and Jeremy Bentham argued that ethical judgments should be more like mathematical operations—universal maxims and formulae in which human variables (equally valued) are processed and calculated. The utilitarians argued, for example, that we should always behave such that we maximize the greatest happiness for the greatest number of people. We today are still heavily influenced by this mathematical model of egalitarian ethics. But Aristotle had a more nuanced view of justice—one that could admit favoritism. We don't have to put our tribal biases in deep storage in order to enter into moral commerce with others. This introduces more ambiguity into our pursuit of justice, because it admits deep asymmetries in our values.[24] The claims of justice are different, Aristotle said, depending on who is involved in the case. "It is a more terrible thing to defraud a friend than a fellow citizen, more terrible not to help a brother than a stranger, and more terrible to wound a father than anyone else."[25]

People often associate bias with bigotry and prejudice, but this is only the worst application of a normal instinct. And the political interpretation usually prevents a more reasoned consideration of favoritism. One of the positive aspects of praising favoritism is that it will afford us an opportunity to examine some virtues that have fallen out of favor in the official cultural conversation—virtues like loyalty, devotion, allegiance, and even attachment. No one wants to be "victim" of someone else's biases, but almost everyone is comforted by the idea that one's brother, mother, or uncle is heavily biased in their favor. Freud reminds us that "my love is valued by all my own people as a sign of my preferring them, and it is an injustice to them if I put a stranger on a par with them."[26]

If Kongzi's example of a sheep-stealing father is the relatively painless or easy ethical case, let's consider the harder case of Euthyphro's father. In the dialogue Euthyphro, Plato records (or stages) a meeting

Fig. 4. Socrates (c. 470–399 BC) was shocked by Euthyphro's willingness to prosecute his own father. Drawing by Stephen Asma.

between Socrates and the very earnest and pious Euthyphro. They run into each other outside the courts. Socrates is on his way to the hearings about his own "impiety"—charges that eventually led to his famous execution. Euthyphro, Socrates discovers, is vigorously pursuing a legal case against his own father.

Socrates is astonished to find the young Euthyphro prosecuting his father. Even when he learns that the charge is *murder*, he ironically cries, "By the powers, Euthyphro! How little does the common herd know of the nature of right and truth. A man must be an extraordinary man, and have made great strides in wisdom, before he could have seen his way to bring such an action." To which Euthyphro arrogantly replies, "Indeed, Socrates, he must." As he struggles to process this indictment, Socrates hits on a speculation that would make some sense of it. "I suppose that the man whom your father murdered was one of your relatives—clearly he was; for if he had been a stranger you would never have thought of prosecuting him." In a contest of bafflement, Euthyphro is now taken aback. "I am amused, Socrates, at your making a distinction between one who is a relation and one who is not a relation; for surely, the pollution is the same in either case."

Euthyphro is bringing a charge of manslaughter because his father left one of his workers, bound and gagged, in a ditch. The worker was bound and gagged because he had, in a drunken fit, killed a servant. Euthyphro's father bound the worker and sent word for religious counsel, but during the wait the man died from "the effect of cold and hunger and chains upon him." Now Euthyphro, over the protests and pleas of his whole family, is prosecuting his father for the crime. Euthyphro's family insists that a son who prosecutes his own father is an impious disgrace. "Which shows," Euthyphro confidently assures Socrates, "how little they know what the gods think about piety and impiety."[27] Euthyphro lays out a notion of justice that respects no persons—an absolute, objective, transcendent tribunal. Socrates shrugs at Euthyphro's naïveté throughout the dialogue. And while no real refutation is stated, the mocking sardonic characterization of Euthyphro and the storm of skeptical queries prevail as a strangely powerful critique. As usual, especially in the early dialogues, Plato's lesson seems to be "Don't be so cocksure of yourself." But he's also bequeathed us an ethical challenge.

Would you prosecute your father for manslaughter? How about murder? How far will you take your favoritism? Does the love you have for your father trump the legal obligation? Do your filial connections override principles of justice? Do those more abstract principles preexist (in God's mind or in the social contract) and thereby supersede your family bonds? Or, as in the case of Confucian ethics, do all the principles of justice (including the political) evolve out of filial piety?

These two paterfamilias cases, Kongzi's and Plato's, do not admit straightforward resolution. They both draw out intuitions about favoritism and ethics, and we will return to them throughout this book. But as you might have guessed by now, I'm no fan of Euthyphro's righteous piety. If *my* dad killed somebody, I don't think I could prosecute him. Of course, if my dad was the bound and gagged worker, who *your* dad killed, well . . . I'd be absolutely eloquent about principled justice and the law (and failing that, I'd be assembling my vigilante options). Where you stand on these cases has less to do with your principles of fairness, and more to do with how and to whom you are tied.[28]

My goals in this book are threefold. First, I wish to more accurately define favoritism and demonstrate its prevalence in our daily lives—revealing how it is a source of virtue and value (even when its subtle melody is usually out-screeched by the one-note song of fairness). Second, though there is much that is good about fairness, I wish to *recommend* favoritism instead, showing why we ought to embrace many of our current preferential tendencies and how we might further educate and refine these tendencies. As Cicero said, "Society and human fellowship will be best served if we confer the most kindness on those with whom we are most closely associated."[29] Lastly, I will ask how we balance, even if precariously, the impulses of fairness and favoritism in an increasingly cosmopolitan world.

2

To Thy Own Tribe Be True
Biological Favoritism

Socrates and Kongzi thought it was shameful to hand over one's father to the judicial system, even if he deserved it. When I asked my own father whether he would surrender *his* dad or shelter him—if he had murdered someone—there was a long pause.

"Well," he finally said, "I'm not sure. I'm inclined, I guess, to turn him in. But, then again, it's a weird question for me, because I never really knew my father. If I had been raised by him and had a good relationship, I would probably shelter him from the law. As it is, he's a bit of a stranger to me."

My dad's father was killed in 1947 when his car was hit by a train. Apparently the crossing guard on duty that night had too much to drink and passed out, unable to lower the guardrail for passing cars. My grandfather was thrown from his car, languished in the hospital for three weeks, and then died on Easter Sunday when my dad was still quite young.

When I asked my father to put himself into the Euthyphro thought experiment, he confessed that he didn't have the requisite feelings about his own father. Without the strong emotional bond with his father, he could see himself—like Euthyphro—going to court against him. Despite his detachment, however, he still hesitated and felt uncomfortable violating even a nominal filial piety.

My mother was more definitive and unforgiving in her answer, as was her usual style. "No, problem," she blurted out, without hesitation. "I'd turn in my father if he murdered someone." I was startled by the speed and zeal of her response. Reading the distaste on my face, she quickly followed with "Well . . . wrong is *wrong*." My father gently reminded her that she did not have any affection for her parents.

"Well," I ventured, "what if *I* had murdered someone?" Here she paused awhile. The look of distaste returned to my face. "That's different," she finally said. I half expected her to start weighing which of her three children she'd narc on and which of us she'd protect.

My mom had been adopted when she was three weeks old by a couple who were teetering on the verge of divorce. They gambled on the idea that a child would glue them back together again, and so my mom was acquired like a desperate hand of blackjack. It didn't work. Her adoptive father was gone within a year, and her adoptive mother embarked on an extended hunt for a new husband. My mom was raised mostly by her aunt (her adoptive mother's sister), and eventually her adoptive mother remarried a quiet navy officer named Raymond. The three strangers then lived under the same roof, in quiet isolation, until my mom was old to enough to leave home. Her parents, my grandparents, were shadowy figures as I grew up. My mother's parents were family in name only.

"It's true, I suppose," my mom confessed to herself, forgetting for a moment that we were even in the room. "I didn't love my parents, because they weren't good to me. But I love my kids," she said, turning back to me, "and that makes all the difference in your little murder example."

Moral Gravity

Why am I going on and on about murderous fathers? Because I think my "little murder example" is a very compelling case study that forces us to think about how far we might go in the service of favoritism. Families are usually the first favorites we have; they serve as the template for many of our later partialities. But as the two different cases of my parents suggest, family membership does not automatically engender the internal feelings of love that bind them and create favorites. For my mother, her parents were not centers of gravity for her, but her own children were—still are, I'm happy to report.

Gravity is a good metaphor. Some people in our lives take on great "affection mass" and bend our continuum of values into a solar system of biases. Family members usually have more moral gravity—what Robert Nozick calls "ethical pull."[1] But modern ethical theory doesn't know what to do with varied degrees of ethical pull. Unequal variables don't fit well in the calculus of rights and duties.

Peter Singer, the famous utilitarian philosopher, believes that the best way to decide between competing pulls is by using an impartial calculation. Singer describes a scenario in which he is about to go out to dinner with three friends, but then his father calls. The father is sick and would like his son to come visit. Singer explains, "To decide impartially I must sum up the preferences for and against going to dinner with my friends, and those for and against visiting my father. Whatever action satisfies more preferences, adjusted according to the strength of preferences, that is the right action I should take."[2]

If his father feels more disappointment at being left alone than he and his three friends feel pleasure at dinner, then Singer is willing to go visit his dad. In the thought experiment, Singer imagines such strong disappointment in his father, and then finally feels justified in abandoning the dinner.

According to this bloodless approach, Singer's father gets no special status just for being his father. Presumably, Singer's father did the usual work of parenting (e.g., raising baby Singer, caring for little Singer when sick, feeding little Singer, sheltering him, nurturing him, etc.). These devotions, according to utilitarians, don't win extra moral gravitas for parents, and feelings of affection between parents and children don't win moral gravitas either.

Singer praises a parent, Zell Kravinsky, who seems to have as much concern for the well-being of strangers as for his own children. Singer implies that this "new standard of giving" is not "defective parenting" (as some suggest), but praiseworthy. After all, sacrificing your own child for the greater good is something, Singer reminds us, that we "accept" in the biblical story of Abraham and Isaac. The moral equality of strangers makes demands on our biased commitments, and vice versa.[3]

In the case of his father, Singer implies that when he adds up preferences (and adjusts according to strengths), the summation will tip the balance toward his father. But he doesn't say this definitively, and he quickly leaves the example with nothing but a vague provisional nod toward a computational solution. It's also very hard to know exactly *what* Singer is adding up here, and how he's *adjusting for strength*. He seems to be saying that the decision will be impartial (and therefore correct) after he's added up his partialities and taken the sum. This approach seems perplexing because it pretends, in its mathematical pretensions, to go beyond subjectivities like "love" and "affection," but then it wants to return them through some back door—with talk of differentially adjusted "strengths" of preference and his father's "disappointment."

This utilitarian approach (the greatest good for the greatest number) can be pushed to its logical conclusion. The hard-core version asserts that it is more ethical to deny your elderly father expensive health care if the same money could save ten starving African strangers. From some utterly impartial, detached perspective (some fictional God's-eye perspective), I suppose this position is "rational." But most of us, saints notwithstanding, are wonderfully partial and irrevocably *attached*.

It's also common for egalitarian moralists to explain the heavier moral gravity of family, by saying that we have the same equal duty to *all* human beings but that the *proximity* of my family makes helping my father much easier than helping the starving African child. This sheer proximity is often taken as useful criteria for solving dilemmas of competing obligations. I want to suggest, however, that favoritism goes beyond such practical or expedient issues—we really *owe* more to our favorites, and not just because of their convenient locations.

In this chapter, I will take an alternative approach to filial favoritism. I will show how such favoritism is originally generated by the development of normal affection in mammals. I will argue that biological bonding is the root system for understanding the ethical pull of favorites. Nepotism has a chemistry that neuroscience is only recently starting to understand. And I will suggest that these data bring us toward a more emotionally based, rather than rationally based, ethics.

Ethicists like Singer tend to contrast the egocentric moral framework with the allocentric framework. The egocentric approach is, of course, the pursuit of those things that are good for the individual self, while allocentric means "centered on others." Since philosophy has had a hard time deriving an other-centered ethic from an egocentric starting place, it has generally characterized egocentrism as the infantile natural default of human beings—but a default that must be corrected by rational allocentric civilization.

However, this starting place seems quite wrongheaded to me, as I will endeavor to show. I will suggest that the allocentric perspective is not derived, but primordial. We are tribal-centric (allocentric) first, and then later learn both to expand this moral circle and ego-identify as we grow. Utilitarians like Singer try to build an other-centered (allocentric) ethic on rational "objective" principles, but they end up with a view that is nemocentric—centered on nobody.

An ideal *centerless view* of the good may be just the thing for certain legal policy considerations, but not in our daily lives. Ethicists who argue the utility of the egalitarian ideal—the practical cost-benefit advantage of treating everyone equally—should at least consider favoritism from the same charitable perspective. In other words, if an ethics of nemocentrism (being centered on nobody) is still considered serviceable and successful despite its occasional flaws, misapplications, and even incoherences, then favoritism also should be forgiven some of its lapses and blunders if it is serviceable in our daily lives.

Obviously, I think Peter Singer and the other utilitarians should get out of their heads, make apologies to their dinner companions and the Africans, and get straight over to see their sick dads. But why do some parents and children bond together as favorites, and some do not? Without sounding too reductionistic, the answer might be brain opioids and oxytocin.

The Biochemistry of Favoritism

I've done a fair amount of fishing in my time, but while I've reeled many fish to shore over the years, I've never seen other fish try to rescue their unfortunate hooked companions. Fish don't rescue each other. Contrast this lack of fish succor with the amazing rescue efforts of whales, dolphins, and other cetaceans. Whales will even form protective circles around their harpooned companions to protect them from whalers. And dolphins have rescued companions from entangled fishing nets.[4]

Fish don't have favorites in the same sense that mammals, like dolphins, do. The evolution of mammals (punctuated in the Paleocene epoch) brought in new emotional bonding equipment. Stronger bonds between kin and clan facilitated sophisticated social emotions like sympathy—a sensitivity to the distress of kin—and favoritism behaviors (like rescue, grooming, consolation behavior, alliance behavior, and so on). It is these emotional ingredients, not rational calculation, that eventually give rise to our ethical lives.

Family bonding is a very complex phenomenon, especially in big-brained humans, but its roots are in the older limbic, or mammal, brain. Social mammals have a neurological process that brain scientists have recently identified and studied. We've known about the phenomenon of vertebrate *imprinting* for many years. Behavioral scientists, working on animals, have described and successfully manipulated this simple form of bonding for decades. Researchers can get baby birds, for example, to imprint on the scientists themselves, on beach balls, and even on beer bottles. This is because a "window" of bonding opens right after birth and closes quickly, so whatever proximate thing is nearby becomes "mom." Mammals have the same, albeit much more sophisticated, mechanisms for fastening together parents and offspring. But only recently have researchers experimentally tracked the neurochemistry of bonding.

Dr. Jaak Panksepp is the founding father of affective neuroscience, a school of brain science that studies the neurochemical pathways of animal emotions—and by extension, human emotions.[5] He calls this neurochemical pathway of mother-child bonding, the CARE system.[6]

And it can be distinguished experimentally from other core emotional affect systems, like FEAR, LUST, SEEKING, PLAY, PANIC, and RAGE— each of which has a uniquely identifiable neurochemical substrate and functional pathway through the brain. Humans have a lot of big-brain flexibility with these biological feelings, but these feelings (part chemical, part psychological) make up the genetically determined operating systems of mammal emotions. Humans share this operating system with other mammals.

Mother-baby bonding is an essential skill for any animal born into a hostile environment. Prey animals, especially herd animals, are born with remarkable physical adeptness. They can walk and even run within minutes of birth. This mobility is important in a predator-filled world, but it puts them at great risk of potential separation from their mothers. So, it's not surprising that herd animals have very tight windows of opportunity for identifying their mothers and latching on.. Other animals—like rats, humans, and predators—have protracted periods of bonding; the window for latching on to mom closes very slowly. Failure to lock on to mom (for any mammal species) usually means death for the offspring and possible termination of the gene line for the parents. So the natural selection pressures for bonding are intense.

Nature has not left bonding up to chance, nor has it waited for rational deliberation or identification to evolve (i.e., many animals are great at bonding, despite an utter lack of intelligence). Instead, internal chemical changes spike during the window of opportunity in the brains and bodies of parents and offspring, cementing them together in ways that are incomparable with other relationships.

Specific neuropeptides—oxytocin, opiates like endorphins, and prolactin—all rise profoundly in the last days of a mother's pregnancy. Oxytocin, sometimes referred to as the "love hormone," regulates several aspects of maternal biology (facilitating labor and breastfeeding), but also plays a crucial role in nurturing behavior—the CARE system. Simply introducing these neuropeptides in high doses into a non-pregnant female mammal will actually produce mothering behaviors. Non-pregnant female rats were given blood transfusions from females who had just given birth, and they immediately began engaging in new maternal behaviors (e.g., building nests, gathering another mother's dispersed pups together, hovering over them to provide warmth, etc.).[7]

Many mammals (and terrestrial vertebrates generally) imprint through the Jacobson's organ (vomeronasal organ) at the roof of the mouth. Chemicals from offspring are taken up by the mother's Jacobson's organ (through smell or oral contact), usually during the cleaning of the just-born baby, and signals are conducted upstream to target sites in the amygdala and hypothalamus. Humans have a vestigial Jacobson's organ, observable in our embryonic phase but largely inactive in adulthood. Different species have diverse ways of harvesting the chemical information that bonds them together, but for mammals the resulting brain chemistry of oxytocin is strikingly similar.

Oxytocin bonding is a time-sensitive process. Sheep have a very short window for the mother to bond with offspring, only an hour or two. If a lamb is removed from its mother for two hours, the mother will not be bonded and will subsequently reject the lamb. But the astonishing thing is that after the bonding window has closed, scientists can *reopen* it again for a couple hours by injecting oxytocin into the mother's brain. Once oxytocin is flooding the system again, the mother can lock on to her offspring and engage in maternal behaviors.[8]

Oxytocin is more than a lever or switch for turning on motherhood. Found only in mammals, oxytocin was one of the first neuropeptides to be isolated and sequenced.[9] Its presence in the breasts (letting down milk) is well known, but more recently scientists have been studying its role in the brain (it's made in the hypothalamus, stored in the posterior pituitary, and then released into circulation). Discovery of oxytocin receptors in the brain signify that the brain is also a target organ for oxytocin. As Dr. Panksepp explains, we now know that oxytocin "reduces all forms of aggression that have been studied." It is, among other things, a general anxiety reducer. Oxytocin calms down aggression and dramatically reduces irritability—important mood alterations for new parents who are often deprived of a good night's sleep. Male moods are equally transformed by oxytocin, which floods the male brain after sex.[10] Male mammals become more nurturing and less aggressive after sex.[11]

Humans Are Wired for Favoritism

In short, oxytocin is a hormone that helps the brain form attachments. It is crucial in early social bonding for mammals. One might object here that I've reduced human bonding to simple rat chemistry. It's common for us to look down our noses at any rodent-human connection, but such condescension about our animality seems increasingly quaint in light of the deep similarities in all mammal biology.[12]

Dr. Seth Pollak and other psychologists at the University of Wisconsin, Madison, discovered that oxytocin is absolutely vital in *human* bonding.[13] Researchers wanted to know why some children fail to bond with their parents. Many kids suffer from "attachment disorders," failing to seek comfort in others, even their own families. Using a control group of non-adopted kids, the researchers collected baseline oxytocin (and vasopressin) levels in eighteen four-year-old kids who were adopted from Russian and Romanian orphanages and had a history of neglect.

Dr. Pollak devised a test in which oxytocin levels were checked before and after comfort/play time with parents. The children were held on the laps of their mothers and played a computer game together, engaging in intimate play, like whispering, tickling, petting, and so on. Immediately after this, the pleasurable oxytocin levels spiked in the non-adopted children, but remained the same in the adopted children. It appears that the anxiety-reducing, calming effects of oxytocin have been *primed* in us by our earliest nurturing experiences. If a child is neglected, in an overpopulated orphanage or in a cold family situation, they fail to form the normal attachment chemistry. We don't entirely understand the mechanics yet, but it looks as though early experience with a loving caregiver "wires" the brain to associate a specific person or people with pleasurable, happy states. This association, which is both chemical and psychological, is the template for positive social bonding in later life.[14]

In light of this study, I reflected on my own mother, who felt very little bond with her parents. Had her short time in an orphanage been instrumental in her detachment? No, the story of biological bonding is more complicated. The adopted kids in the study had global problems with attachment—they struggled to bond with anybody and everybody. My mom, like most other adopted kids, was perfectly capable (and demonstrable) in forming all kinds of family and friendship bonds. Her "favoritism abilities," and the abilities of most adopted kids, are not compromised. Being an orphan doesn't make you a cold, detached person. Moreover, there are obviously plenty of mundane events from personal history that drive people away from their parents or other family members.

It turns out that, just as the case of sheep imprinting, humans have an oxytocin-based bonding window of opportunity. Further study of orphaned kids suggests that a child who is adopted young—between birth and approximately eighteen months old—will still have the open window for bonding with her eventual caregivers. Unfortunately, children who are neglected in orphanages for more than this time frame seem to arrive in their new families with the chemical bonding

So it is not only birth mother [handwritten marginalia]

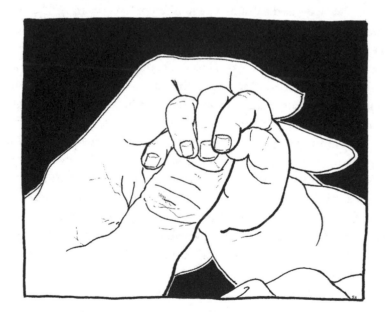

Fig. 5. Humans, like other mammals, have a biochemical bonding process that ties together our first circle of favorites, the nuclear family. This early bonding primes our brains for the attachments of subsequent social life. Drawing by Stephen Asma.

windows *closed*. It appears that these children will always have more difficulty forming strong attachments. Children's brains are changed by the early presence of their parents and vice versa. Families literally prepare the pumps of emotional chemistry and smooth the pathway to later social connection.

The importance of oxytocin in emotional social bonding is further suggested by the fact that autistic individuals, who can be very detached, show only half the oxytocin levels of age-matched controls. Some psychologists are even suggesting oxytocin therapies as a way to improve the social behaviors and emotions of autistics.[15]

A Healthy Addiction

This entire account of biological favoritism is additionally strengthened by the fact that brain-based *opiates* are also heavily triggered by family interactions. Dr. Panksepp experimented on internal brain opiates in dogs, guinea pigs, chickens, and rats, and found them to be crucial in child-mother bonding and in general socialization.

We all have natural pain-killing chemicals akin to heroin and morphine swimming in our brains. And we have receptors to receive these natural neurochemicals, which is why artificial narcotic versions can key their way into our moods, emotions, and our subjective consciousness. Having some level of opioid activity in our brains produces a pleasurable equanimity, even euphoric, steady state, or homeostasis.[16] They make us feel happy. Affective neuroscientists, studying both animals and humans, have shown that social interaction increases opioid production in the brain. I get high with a little help from my friends.

Low opioid levels actually goad us into seeking out other people. Separation distress in animals that are removed from their mothers or their group can be immediately reduced by the introduction of opioids. Positive social interaction for mammals seems to derive much of its pleasure from the opioid release that accompanies it. Opioid systems go into overdrive during juvenile animal play and during social grooming in older mammals. If we don't get good opioid levels, we seek out social interactions like a junkie looking for his next fix. We are literally addicted to other people.

Everyone knows that being around their favorite people is pleasurable, but now we understand that our favorite people are actually triggering internal brain narcotics. Your favorite people feel good to be around—they contribute to brain homeostasis—and that is a crucial explanation of why these people have a very high preferential value.[17] Most of these unconscious processes are inaccessible to our conscious minds, but they're profoundly influential on our daily moods, values, and behaviors.

We've known about the *correlations* of mammal behaviors for decades, but not much about the *causes* until now. Henry Harlow's famous experiments with rhesus monkeys, in the early 1960s, showed us tragically how babies without comforting mothers go insane, even if their other needs are fully met. And decades of behaviorism, with primates starving themselves to death for another hit of cocaine, have shown us the obvious correlations between pleasure and behavior. But affective neuroscience actually shows us how and why these correlations are regularly observed. Brain homeostasis and the feedback of pleasure chemistry are at the root of our pursuit for social bonding.

All this suggests something profound. Yes, we already knew that we're biased in favor of our families—that's not breaking news. What seems radical here is that our *brains* are actually biased toward our families.[18] My young developing brain has neurochemical changes in the presence of my nurturing family members, changes that do not happen with associates, coworkers, and strangers.[19] "Not only do we simply feel better about those we already know than we do strangers," Dr. Panksepp says, "but even their faces, voices, and ways of being are engraving more powerful affective imprints in our memories."[20] Or as writer George Eliot puts it: What greater thing is there for human souls than to feel that they are joined for life—to be with each other in silent unspeakable memories?[21]

The parent-child bond is the first big, chemically underwritten, gravitational pull in our system of values. And the positive feelings of those bonds (the affective emotions) reach out beyond mere subjective states, eventually motivating real preferential *action* in the public world.[22]

I want to suggest something bold and ironic here. It looks like the original source of all our pro-social behavior (no matter how wide the circle) is our very particular early attachments. This means that even the pro-social "fairness" of liberalism may be psychologically dependent on the very unfair early bonds of parents and children. If this is true, then we must be careful not to extend our liberal aspirations of disinterested fairness too far, because we might undermine the very mechanisms that give rise to them when people are mature enough to connect affect to principle. It may be that only early childhood favoritism triggers the pro-social biochemistry that we'll need if we are to be genuinely concerned with fairness later in life.[23] Too strident a cultural rejection of bias and favoritism might well be producing a whole society of attachment-disordered citizens whose nominal dedication to egalitarianism may be only skin-deep.

Armed now with some understanding of the biochemistry of bonding, what do we make of those "favoritism cases" from Kongzi and Socrates? Is Euthyphro willing to roll over on his dad because he's more principled or because he failed to get enough oxytocin/opioid feelings with his father? How should we conceptualize this case? One way— Euthyphro's way—is to see failure to prosecute his father as a failure of moral piety (a view of absolute duty). From the viewpoint I've been sketching, however, the failure to stay loyal to his father might be a pathological failure of bonding (a glitch in the biochemistry of filial love). I will argue later that there is a notable correlation between filially detached personalities and strident egalitarianism.

Obviously, between the motivating poles of *absolute principles* and *biochemistry* lay other motivations, like conscious psychology, social expectations, and so on. But I'm trying to isolate the genesis of certain nepotistic feelings—affects that are more unconscious than conscious. Freudian explanations of unconscious filial devotion, with unfalsifiable Oedipal machinations, have been deeply unsatisfying.[24] Now it's neuroscience's turn. The results that are trickling in, like the ones I've been sketching, look more promising.

Philosophers generally avoid such psychologizing arguments. Is it ad hominem to suggest that Euthyphro's moral decision resulted from the possibility that he didn't love his father? Is it unfair to suggest that his position is flawed because he himself is flawed? My argument may be ad hominem in the sense that it looks to the man's personal biography, but I don't think the argument is fallacious. If the real motive behind a moral action is a *feeling* (e.g., empathy, care, etc.) rather than a *principle*, then exploring the emotional makeup of the agent is absolutely essential for evaluating his particular actions. Moreover, if the law and our moral intuitions consider compromised cognitive abilities (e.g., mental retardation) relevant for questions of culpability, then we may need to start including *affective* deficiencies in our assessments of moral action.

Flexible Favoritism

Given these data, an interesting puzzle arises about kids who grow up with the ability to bond with other people, but who don't feel bonded with their parents. The example of my mother is useful again. If parent bonding is the first template, then how does my mother, who approves of narcing on her own parents, become positively "lioness" about me or others to whom she's bonded?

Two scenarios suggest themselves, but these may not be exhaustive options. One, a kid may receive all the biochemical defaults set by caregiving parents—the oxytocin/opioid defaults for future friendships/romances etc.—but then subsequent events (real or even perceived injuries from the parents) lead the grown child to reject the parents.

Frank Calabrese Jr. actually turned evidence against his own father, mob boss Frank Calabrese Sr., in 2007. The father appears to have been a loathsome character who preyed upon anyone, including his own family. Frank Jr. describes how the very first thing he felt when he entered the courtroom to testify against his father (whom he hadn't seen in five years) was an overwhelming desire to go hug him. But this was quickly followed by all the feelings of dread, fear, and hatred that his father usually inspired. Frank Jr. explained: "I loved my father. I love him dearly to this day. But I don't love his ways. I just didn't understand why he didn't have mine and my brother's backs. . . . He'd never have our backs. We'd always have his back. I was willing to kill and die for this man."[25]

One wonders, in cases of bonding breakdown, if the old pleasurable chemistry rises up unconsciously in the grown child when put in proximity with the parents (and this is a scientifically testable hypothesis). Or are oxytocin levels squelched by overriding rational judgments of injustice and/or other negative affective stressors (e.g., drops in serotonin levels, spikes in testosterone, cortisol, etc.)? The periaqueductal gray of the midbrain appears to integrate the biochemistries of anger, defense, or attack. It's possible that this rage system is triggered by memories of previous slights, insults, or abuses (perceived or real), and this strong response overrides the more original bonding system of the infant stage. With this option, the parent has successfully engendered the abilities of bonding in their child but can no longer enjoy the fruits of that ability.[26]

The second possible explanation of people like my mother is that a child may have had cold or even abusive parents and failed to form any default warmth from that interaction, but someone else in close proximity (e.g., a doting aunt, uncle, sibling, etc.) may have unknowingly built the ability in the otherwise deprived infant. Many badly parented kids will attest in later life to the emotional life-preserver that one or two other relations provided them.

The flexibility of biological bias is a crucial point. The brain is not wired in the deterministic way we once thought, where genes just build the brain mechanically and the machine expresses itself out toward the environment. Instead, plasticity or malleability is the rule for developing brains.[27] Default biases get engraved into the brain, but those defaults are relative to particular environmental experiences (an adoptive parent is engraved just as deeply as a blood parent, if the nurturing happens within the child's bonding timetable). Moreover, our unique neocortical powers (our high-level autobiographical rational minds) can direct and redirect some of these affective biases (feelings of favoritism) all through our subsequent lives. In other words, our bias defaults do not set like cement (as they probably do for some animals) but remain open to new experiences. This will prove crucial as we later consider how far nuclear bonding can be stretched to accommodate strangers.

Kin Selection

Darwinian natural selection edits and shapes populations by favoring or deleting individual traits, according to their adaptive utility in a specific environment. The *unit* or subject of the selection process is complicated. Darwin emphasized the individual organism as the unit of selection. My dog is fitter than your dog, for example, to survive on the frozen tundra, and so the hostile environment edits your dog (and subsequent gene line) out of the picture. Biologist Richard Dawkins famously argued that the *gene*, not the organism, is the proper unit of selection. Yes, my individual dog lives and yours dies in the above scenario, but nature is selecting *against* the genetic variation that produces a thin wispy coat of hair and *for* the genes that generate a thick woolly coat. Our dogs just happen to be carrying these respective genes. Naturalist Stephen Jay Gould, ever the pluralist, argued that natural selection operates at both levels—organisms and genes—and many points in-between.

In addition to selection working *below* the level of the organism, we have come to understand (since the 1960s) that selection also works *above* the individual—at the level of the social group.[28] Natural selection at the level of family or genetic community is called kin selection, and it is one of the driving engines of social evolution.[29] Many social animals, besides ourselves, set aside their selfish urges to engage in altruistic behaviors (like social grooming, food sharing, protection, and task cooperation). Kin selection is a way to understand how seemingly "disadvantaging behavior" could have invisible but powerful genetic advantages.

Social insects, like ants or bees, are good examples of groups that flourish even when some individuals are disadvantaged (e.g., workers are sterile and have no way to pass on their genes directly, but their larger gene pool—the hive or colony—benefits from their many sacrifices). Or ground squirrels, for example, that call out alert chirps to warn their companions of an impending threat can save a clan of squirrels, but the chirp itself brings the predator's attention to the chirper. How could altruistic behavior be selected for if natural selection only operated at the level of each individual? Chirping would be wiped out quickly, unless the family of related squirrels benefited substantially and lived on to procreate the virtually same gene pool (including the altruistic chirping trait). As Stephen Jay Gould puts it, "By benefitting relatives, altruistic acts preserve an altruist's genes even if the altruist himself will not be the one to perpetuate them."[30] These cases are just the hard cases (extreme altruism) that prove the rule: kin will frequently compromise their own advantage in favor of their relatives.[31]

When biologists Paul Sherman and John Hoogland studied ground

Fig. 6. Ground squirrels and prairie dogs chirp warning signals to their clan when they perceive nearby danger. The squirrel's warning cries are louder and more frequent if its direct family members are close by and under threat. Drawing by Stephen Asma.

squirrel and prairie dog calling behaviors, they independently confirmed that warning calls become much more frequent and intense when kin are nearby.[32] Animals will also engage in "rescue missions" against predators, if their own relatives have been captured or cornered. In short, preferential behaviors—stemming from biological favoritism— can be lifesaving behaviors. Attachments must be uniquely intense— etched in the mammal family experience—if they are to compete with an animal's egocentric tendencies. Presumably blood nepotism evolved first, and this chemically based behavior developed into wider (non-blood) networks of social cohesion.[33]

The correlations of kin selection have been known for decades. The old joke is that I'll throw myself on a hand grenade for two brothers or eight cousins—and population geneticists have actually worked out mathematical models of kin selection over time. But now, through affective neuroscience, we are beginning to understand the emotional or affective springs that trigger the behaviors associated with kin selection (at least for mammals). I don't do a rational calculation when a hand grenade falls in the room, still less does a prairie dog do math to figure out if it should chirp more warnings when its siblings are nearby. The engines of nepotistic action are not rational but emotional or chemical.[34]

Rational or Emotional Motives

Your emotional brain, the limbic system, is a natural nepotist. Your rational neocortex, however, is much more *principled*. The idea that everyone deserves equal treatment, that everyone has equal claim upon resources, or that everyone has equal value as my kin are all foreign to the intrinsically hierarchical emotional brain. This is because our experience-based *values* (whether it is a valuable object, person, or idea) are originally encoded in the course of psychological development by *feelings* (e.g., chemically grounded oxytocin, opioid, or dopamine patterns).

The biological process of filial favoritism is a *pattern* or a *happening*— a mammalian *tendency*, not a principle. My own view is that many high principles take their start from lowly patterns or tendencies, but our smart neocortical rationalizations abstract these principles out of the more humble experiential patterns. By this process, an affective experience of bonding with my favorites can be inductively extrapolated into a rough-and-ready rule of action—a principle we might call *loyalty*. Now could this extrapolation continue up the social domains to generate a rule of general *reciprocity*? The Romans used to say, "*Do ut des,*" or "I give, so that you will give." And then could this "I'll scratch your back . . ." rule of thumb evolve further into a depersonalized egalitarian principle?[35]

The answers to these questions may be forthcoming in the future (as we blend neurophilosophy, social psychology, and anthropology), but one thing that's clear from the biology of bias is this: we don't come into the world as selfish Hobbesian mercenaries. Contrary to the usual pessimistic contract theory, we mammals don't start out as self-serving egotistical individuals who then need to be socialized (through custom, reason, and law) to endure the compromises of tribal living.[36] Rather, we start out in a sphere of emotional-chemical values—created by family care—in which feelings of altruistic bonding are preset before the individual ego even extricates itself.

Freud's famous assumption *Homo homini lupus* (man is a wolf to other men) not only tries to posit the isolated aggressive interests of the early ego phase, but also the artificial nature of morality itself. Biologist Frans de Waal calls this the "veneer theory" because "it sees morality as a cultural overlay, a thin veneer hiding an otherwise selfish and brutish nature."[37] De Waal contrasts this veneer theory with the Darwinian view that morality is a "natural outgrowth of the social instincts, hence continuous with the sociality of other animals." The story I've been telling about ancient emotional kin bonding dovetails with this Darwinian view that moral sentiments are early and foundational for both individual and species ethics.

Obviously, I think there is an ancient favoritism instinct, and it's not the usual individualistic selfish instinct that veneer theorists might call "human nature." It's a tribal instinct that has altruism already built in (caring and being cared for are intrinsically, even intoxicatingly rewarding). But I do not wish to suggest that a *favoritism instinct* renders *fairness* as a mere figment. We are finding more and more that there is a *fairness instinct* as well.

Food sharing is quite normal between mammal mothers and off-

spring, but rare across other social relationships. Chimpanzees and ca-
puchin monkeys, however, have been shown to engage in some recip-
rocal sharing between friends or allies. More interestingly, they also
seem to have a keen sense of fairness—as it applies to the distribution
of food. Primatologists Frans de Waal and Sarah Brosnan trained capu-
chin monkeys to perform a bartering task. Two capuchins, in adjacent
cages, were trained to take a token from a trainer and then trade the
token back for a piece of food. Each monkey could easily witness the
barter of the other. The food reward for this barter was usually a slice
of cucumber, which capuchins like to eat. But grapes are universally
loved by capuchins as a delicacy. If one monkey bartered her token
and received only a cucumber slice, but then watched as the other
monkey received a grape for the same kind of token, the first monkey
would become incensed—refusing to play on, throwing tokens back
at the experimenter, protesting, and even punishing the lucky grape
recipient.[38]

Having expectations about resource distributions and having aversion to inequity probably evolved in social animals that cooperate to
secure food. Of course, *detecting* fairness and *being* fair are two different things, but at least some primates seem to have a natural ability for
this rudimentary morality.

My suspicion, however, is that this kind of mammalian fairness is
a latecomer on the evolutionary stage. Hierarchically arranged animal
groups would distribute food on a different model than egalitarianism.
Dominant animals get more, and subordinates get less—that is a kind
of fairness that we recognized in chapter 1 as a kind of meritocracy
notion of deserts. Presumably dominant animals do more to further
the survival of the group. But even before this early social system of
resource distribution, blood ties must have trumped most competing
claims on resources. I suspect that true fairness developed in tandem
with the cognitive advances of primate neocortical evolution.[39]

Conflicting Brain Systems

One tantalizing piece of evidence that suggests both the emotive foundation of ethics and the primacy of favoritism is the vMPC brain-scan

study. The VMPC, ventromedial prefrontal cortex, regulates emotions (among other things) and works in intimate communication with the ancestral limbic system. Brain-scan technology is being mixed with old-school philosophy dilemmas to reveal some very interesting insights.

The classic trolley-car ethics experiment is well known to many. It's a thought experiment that asks you to imagine yourself on a bridge overlooking a speeding trolley car that's hurtling toward a group of five unaware pedestrians. The track splits in two directions, and you have the track-switching lever in front of you. You can, if you act in time, switch the trolley onto the other track, avoiding the deaths of the five pedestrians. But the alternate track has one pedestrian walking un-awares, and he will certainly die if you do the switch. So, what do you do? Save the many and kill the one? Leave it to run its own course? These and countless other lifeboat scenarios and thought experiments are designed to reveal our ethical intuitions. Most people, it turns out, will try to maximize the greatest good for the greatest number. They'll crunch the utilitarian calculus and throw the switch to save the five pedestrians.

The outcomes of the thought experiment change radically, however, when you replace the lone track-walker with your brother or sister, mother or father, or even best friend. The guy on the other track is not some abstract stranger, but one of your own favorite people. Now the utilitarian solution unravels quickly. Most people cannot overcome their biases in order to "do the right thing" (in the utilitarian sense).

Neuroscientists started scanning brain activity of subjects who were posed these ethical dilemmas, and definite patterns emerged. When a patient's VMPC is normal, they almost always answer the ethical dilemmas in favor of their *favorites*, not in favor of the *majority*. Healthy emotional VMPC subjects are guided by their biases. But if the emotional VMPC is damaged, the subject becomes extremely utili-tarian (hyper-rational) in their responses. Emotionally compromised subjects have no hesitation (at least in thought experiments) to sac-rifice their own kin for the greater good. Citing studies in *Neuron* and *Nature*, William Saletan states that scanning technology reveals a correspondence between utilitarian ethics and the cognitive control

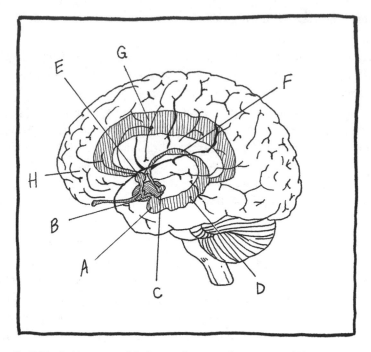

Fig. 7. The limbic system of the brain is the nexus of our emotional life. It privileges our associations, codes our experience, with all manner of bias. (A) amygdala, (B) hypothalamus, (C) mammillary body, (D) hippocampus, (E) septum, (F) fornix, (G) cingulate gyrus, and (H) vmpc. Drawing by Stephen Asma.

systems of the brain. Whereas the older socio-emotional limbic brain, inherited from our mammal ancestors, seems to inform our more biased ethical judgments.[40]

Egalitarian fairness (especially the "disinterested" form) is more cognitive than emotional. It's probably a late outgrowth of tribal reciprocity—which is itself an outgrowth of offspring bonding, and the evolution of kin altruism. Most animals are only "fair" inside their social groups, not outside them. So, *Homo homini lupus* may be a truer slogan than the pessimists think. The pessimistic interpretation—typified by Thomas Hobbes's famous view of nature as a "war of all against all"—should be revised in light of real wolf nature. Wolves can be highly aggressive, but their fierceness is for those *outside* their pack, outside their tribe. Inside their hierarchic pack, they are loyal and semi-altruistic. Wolves (and we) are more tribal-centric than egocentric.

Does that mean we should be animals? No, of course not. We, unlike wolves, can reach beyond genetic programming, and in many cases we should. We can bond with almost any caregiver. Blood is not necessary. And fresh developmental experiences, fresh habits and behaviors, can route and reroute genetic expression (i.e., epigenetic pliability). The system has play and flexibility in it.

Biological favoritism starts as an automatic chemical bonding between parents and offspring, but as our mental sophistication grows, we begin to recognize the subjective feeling of favoritism (philosophers would call this the *phenomenology* of favoritism—how it *feels* to prefer and be preferred). Here I think we recognize many of the emotions that we associate with the moral life: sympathy, empathy, jealousy, love. And it is not enough to simply have emotional tendencies. They

Fig. 8. Wolves can be highly aggressive, but their fierceness is for those *outside* their pack—outside their tribe. Inside their hierarchic pack, they are loyal and less aggressive. They are not egalitarian in their social organization, but neither are they egocentrically selfish loners. Drawing by Stephen Asma.

may be necessary, but they are not sufficient for a healthy ethics. Darwin points out that "sympathy, though gained as an instinct, is also much strengthened by exercise or habit."[41]

Paleoanthropology provides evidence that our ancestors started hoarding together stone tools, food, and other resources at collective sites around 2 million years ago. Around 800,000 years ago, early humans began gathering around hearths, for many purposes, including safety from predators, sharing food, information, comfort, conserving resources, and warmth. Our big-brain explosion occurred around 500,000 years ago (followed by communication with symbols 250,000 years ago, longer childhood and adolescence 160,000 years ago, and plant and animal domestication 10,000 years ago).

A big brain and the development of human culture meant the expansion of small-scale blood ties to larger frames of bias (e.g., friendship). Marriage, or more accurately pair bonding, was just a subset of resource alliance, but it must have been one of the cultural innovations that enlarged the sphere of favoritism beyond blood. In the contemporary developed West, it may be hard to see the purpose of marriage as kin merging and expansion, but throughout the developing world these expedient origins are still obvious.[42]

Our big brains allow us great flexibility beyond blood, but our allegiance groups are still, at the core, "affective communities"—human clusters of shared emotional connection. This will prove to be decisive when I argue, in chapter 6, that our allegiance groups will always remain small.

Facts and Values

All this raises the vexed question of *facts* versus *values*. I have been explaining some emerging biochemical facts about human (and mammal) favoritism. Philosopher David Hume (1711–1776) famously said that we cannot derive an *ought* (a normative statement) from an *is* (a factual statement). Hume had a sophisticated view of the passions and may have agreed even with the idea that a limbic system can transform a perception (*is*) into a motivation (*ought*), but many subsequent philosophers have interpreted Hume's logical is/ought split as a prohibition against ethical naturalism.[43] I cannot share this skepticism about the is/ought problem. I stand with other ethical naturalists, like Aristotle and Darwin, who believed that facts about human biology are relevant for our normative ethical values. If you want to know what is *good* for human beings, Aristotle thought, you don't study *The Good* (as Plato tried). Instead, you study *human beings*.

I'll invoke Aristotle's idea that humans, like other species, have a *nature* or a *telos*. This is usually misunderstood—partly because the medieval schoolmen "baptized" Aristotle's biology and reinterpreted it in a cosmic teleology framework—but Aristotle just meant that each species had natural tendencies or powers or virtues (*areté*), and you could discern what those were by empirically investigating the animal's life. Horses seem built to run, sloths seem built to crawl upside down, human hands built to grasp, fish fins to swim, and so on. Some of these *teloi* or *natures* are species-specific (e.g., all dogs have dichromatic vision—they see in shades of two colors, instead of our three) and some *teloi* apply to larger classes of animals (e.g., all mammals give birth to live young).

"Telos" in this sense should not be interpreted as purpose, because that is very misleading and suggests a Designer metaphysics. Instead, telos is a way of isolating unique natural abilities, tendencies, or predispositions. And—something Aristotle didn't know—we now understand that such predispositions are genetically engraved (albeit with some significant plasticity) over evolutionary time.

My claim is that favoritism is natural for humans in the same way that breastfeeding is natural. Of course, we can always ask: Granted, we do *factually* show preferential favoritism, but *should* we do so? Maybe evolution has constructed us for breastfeeding, but we now wish to culturally break from this practice (because more nutritious options have been discovered, or some such reasoning). Maybe evolution has constructed us for preferential favoritism, but we now wish to break from nepotism and pursue saintly egalitarianism.

The twentieth century certainly saw some social engineering experiments that tried to break the natural biases of family. Mao Zedong in China and Pol Pot in Cambodia, for example, tried to force a radical egalitarianism, but it was a disaster. I suspect that we could try to teach ourselves to be egalitarian in all things (Mao and Pol Pot even tried to break down the nuclear family), but this would be like teaching ourselves to walk on our hands—it *can* be done perhaps, but why not use the powers that evolution has shaped? In this case, why not use the nepotistic affective sentiments themselves as a launching pad for ethical direction?

Obviously, I think that bonding, bias, and even loyalty are biological, but that is not *why* I think they should be respected as virtues. Favoritism is not *good* just because it is natural. I take it as obvious that filial love is intrinsically part of the good life (the happy life of actualized potential), and I don't feel compelled to give arguments for such a self-evident truth. But I also hope to make the case that favoritism can segue into the wider public sphere and do much good there as well. The coming chapters of this book will endeavor to articulate a variety of arguments for why favoritism can be a legitimate good in the larger cosmopolitan ethic.

3

In Praise of Exceptions

If nepotistic favoritism is our natural default value, then how do we develop such hostility toward our biases later in life? How do we go from the (at least partly) biology-based partiality of tribalism to the principled ideology of modern fairness? This is a relevant question for historians, childhood psychologists, and anthropologists. Every contemporary American child learns to value non-kin and strangers, granting them historically unprecedented consideration. So, too, Western liberalism has evolved to recognize and include more strangers inside our sphere of ethical consideration.[1]

In this chapter, I want to tackle the first of two related topics. How did Western culture develop a new ideology of fairness? In the next chapter, I'll consider the kind of nurturing that instills such fairness in our kids—how do our children acquire these same cultural principles and creeds of impartiality?

For most cultural historians and philosophers, the evolution of egalitarianism, from the seventeenth century to the present, has been a stunning success story. But, while I applaud the charity and tolerance enshrined in the usual progress story, I will point out the lost values that fell by the wayside during this long march.

Building the Grid of Impartiality

In Rembrandt's famous *The Syndics of the Drapers' Guild* (1662), we find the classic Dutch group portrait. The painting depicts the board of inspectors for the clothmakers' guild, a sober group of gentlemen that Rembrandt represents as accomplished equals. I first met this painting when I was a kid, on the box cover of my father's Dutch Masters cigars. A cheap cigar company using Rembrandt's portrait as a logo has a fitting irony. The product designers wanted to invoke a stylish aristocratic connotation, lending an elite European sophistication to a mass-produced American stogie. But the choice was more poetic than they probably realized, because Rembrandt's portrait is actually a testament to the new leveling and democratization of seventeenth-century Holland. What better symbol, then, for the everyman's American cigar than a homogenous group of undistinguished but unsubjugated entrepreneurs?

Dutch painting exploded in the seventeenth century, after the Eighty Years' War of independence from Spain (1568–1648). The new Dutch republic—fueled by strong trade, military strength, and scientific advances—quickly became one of the most prosperous parts of the world. Group portraiture, practically a Dutch invention, became very popular during the rise of the new wealthy mercantile class. Civic groups, trustees, militias, scientific societies, and business partners all enjoyed pictorial commemoration, oftentimes splitting the cost of a large portrait and depositing the final painting with the local city council.[2]

This style of pictorial representation was a departure from earlier portraiture that tended to exaggerate the centrality and even size of the patron. Important people were always enlarged to convey the relevant hierarchy. And if we go back a little further in the history of painting—before the rediscovery of Euclidean perspective grids—we find the charming world of medieval painting, where popes and exceptional people are drawn bigger than the commoners, buildings, and

Fig. 9. Rembrandt's *The Syndics of the Drapers' Guild* (1662) typifies the growing
egalitarianism of northern Europe in the seventeenth century. Art, politics, and
ethics became increasingly democratized, in conjunction with the scientific revolution.
Drawing by Stephen Asma, based on the Rembrandt painting.

even mountains. The history of Western painting from the medieval
to the Enlightenment era can be read as the increasing standardiza-
tion of objective proportion. Artists like Albrecht Dürer (1471–1528)
actually started to place new perspective grids in front of his subjects
in order to more accurately measure objective spatial relations. These
were wooden screens crisscrossed by strings that made up a network
of equal squares, preventing the artist from biased representation.
Clergy are not really bigger than householders, just because they are
"closer to God." Kings and royals generally do not possess supernatural physiques, and patrons should not be drawn bigger than workers
just because they're wealthy.

As wealth grew in Holland, so did humanistic tolerance. Increasingly, individuals were at liberty to pursue their own interests without
harassment from the state or the church. A cornerstone of individualism in northern Europe had already been laid by the Protestant
Reformation's critique of Catholic authority. The Peace of Westphalia
and the empowerment of middle-class culture meant that industrious
commoners of low birth could ascend in the new fungible world of pa-

Fig. 10. Italian painter Giotto di Bondone (1266–1337) typifies the pre-egalitarian, pre-objective approach to pictorial space and characters. Important people were bigger than buildings, and God's favorites were further designated by golden halos. Drawing by Stephen Asma, based on Giotto's *Encounter at the Golden Gate* (c. 1306, Padua).

per currency. Paintings, like group portraits or the growing depictions of domestic life, enshrined a new egalitarian ethos. Everyday life, previously thought "vulgar" and unworthy of artistic representation, became the new subject matter of an increasingly democratic society.[3]

It wasn't just painting that began to convey egalitarian ideas. Nature itself, during this era, went from being considered a Great Chain of Being to being viewed as a uniform machine.[4] Around the same time that Dutch artists were democratizing painting, Galileo (1564–1642) was democratizing *matter* itself. Prior to Galileo, Aristotelian cosmology held sway for almost two thousand years. Galileo shifted science from a geocentric (earth-centered) cosmos to a heliocentric (sun-centered)

Fig. 11. A typical pre-modern painting depicting the non-egalitarian "greatness" of its subject (Emperor Otto) and the relative unimportance of other humans. Medieval notions of pictorial perspective reflected theological and political biases, and made no attempt to standardize sizes. Drawing by Stephen Asma, based on a medieval painting of Emperor Otto II (955–983).

solar system—bumping us off our central throne of privilege. We used to be the favorites of the whole universe, and now we were just another of the planets, no more or less special than Mars or Mercury.

Galileo's leveling and mechanizing of nature was even more profound because he upset the old physics and metaphysics division between sub-lunar (our earthly realm, stretching from here to the moon) and supra-lunar (the heavenly realm beyond the moon's orbit). For thousands of years before Galileo, we believed that the earth was composed of four elements (earth, air, fire, and water) and that all motion occurred in straight lines (rectilinear motion). But if you moved up and out of our stratosphere, beyond the moon's orbit, you would find yourself in a totally different physics. Here, the theory went, planets and stars were composed of a different "stuff"—something airy, light, and divine. This fifth element, called "ether," was unlike the changeable four elements. Ether was relatively changeless and explained why the heavens moved in beautiful circular motions, rather than mundane rectilinear motions. For two millennia we believed that the heavens were made of metaphysically different stuff—ether substances, crystalline spheres, and divine agencies. Nature itself was hierarchically arranged in a scale of perfection. The night sky was a visible canvas of the more perfect supernatural world.

Galileo, and then Newton, changed all this. Galileo's telescope revealed a more realistic and less romanticized view of the planets and stars. They appeared, upon closer inspection, to have earthy qualities—the sun had spots and fluctuations, for example, that seemed inconsistent with the ideas of changeless heavenly perfection; Jupiter could be seen to have orbiting moons of its own, and this violated the belief that all heavenly bodies circled earth; and shockingly our moon (which Dante called an "eternal pearl") appeared to have earth-like mountains and craters.

Galileo's astronomy and physics began to unify nature into one giant system of material substances, processes, and laws. Not only were the heavens made of the same stuff as the mundane world, but this ubiquitous stuff all conformed to predictable laws of motion. And Galileo, together with contemporaries like René Descartes and Robert Boyle, also deconstructed the hierarchies of earthly substances by resuscitating the atomic or corpuscular theory of matter. Atomic materialism is the great leveler.[5] Atomism is to metaphysics what democracy is to politics. It treats every substance as intrinsically equal—made of the same stuff; the only real difference between gold and garbage is just varying arrangements of these same atoms.

Isaac Newton (1642–1727) continued this revolution. He demonstrated the universal logic hiding beneath the appearances of diverse nature. Newton's universal gravitation and three laws of motion (the law of inertia; force equals mass times acceleration; and for every action there is an equal and opposite reaction) continued the egalitarianism of matter itself. He showed how the most mundane motions (e.g., I drop my pen) and the most elegant heavenly motions (e.g., the planetary orbits or trajectories of comets) are governed by the same universal natural laws. When Galileo suggested such unified laws, it was considered heretical—a "constraint" upon the free creativity of the deity. But by the time Newton codified such uniform laws, they were interpreted as signs of the deity's rational ingenuity. Alexander Pope famously captured this in his epitaph for Sir Isaac:

> Nature and Nature's laws lay hid in night:
> God said, Let Newton be! And all was light.

Newton's successes in natural philosophy inspired a generation of ethical philosophers who wanted a similar universal and rational logic, a scientific foundation, for human society. Philosophers like David Hume and Adam Smith tried to rethink the moral sentiments as a foundation for building a better culture. Exhausted by religious wars, European intellectuals sought new, objective foundations for building peaceful cosmopolitan societies.[6] Hume and his friend Adam Smith developed sentiment-based theories of ethics—what we now call emotivist ethics.[7] Hume said, "Morals excite passions, and produce or prevent actions. Reason itself is utterly impotent in this particular. The rules of morality, therefore, are not conclusions of our reason."[8]

Let me give an example. Worried that emotions were too subjective, fluctuating, and self-centered to support a science of social life, Adam Smith called for an "impartial spectator" perspective in ethics. If I'm injured and angry, then I'll be too close to the events and feelings to respond in a healthy and ethical way—I'll probably give way to revenge and sadistic impulses. But an impartial spectator will pursue the more appropriate balance of justice. This detached, "disinterested," or "indifferent" perspective helps a person to "harmonize the sentiments and passions," and in this balance lies the "perfection of human nature" and society.[9]

The idea of an impartial spectator survived in the subsequent utilitarian tradition, started by Jeremy Bentham and continued by John Stuart Mill, which tried to formalize and mathematize the sentiment-based ethics of Scottish thinkers like Hume and Smith. In England Jeremy Bentham (1748–1832) tried to formulate a "Pannomion," an all-encompassing system of laws based on the "greatest happiness principle." His approach pushed the impartial spectator idea so far that he ended up depersonalizing it entirely and turned instead toward the idea of an ethical calculator.

Bentham's utilitarian philosophy began from the acknowledgment that "Nature has placed mankind under the governance of two sovereign masters, pain and pleasure. It is for them alone to point out what we ought to do, as well as to determine what we shall do."[10] Bentham claimed that a "hedonic calculus" (pleasure or happiness calculus) could measure the variables of pleasure and pain (the elements) in any decision-making scenario. The calculus postulated vectors like intensity of pleasure or pain, duration, certainty of occurrence, likelihood of recurrence, number of people impacted, and so on.[11]

This sort of utilitarian approach lives on in many of our contemporary fairness philosophies. Systematizing human societies along scientific principles (in this case, using sentiments or feelings) was the beginning of the end of favoritism in the West. The seeds of our opposition to bias and partiality are sown in this Enlightenment era.

But no one tried harder to transform human ethics into Newtonian science than German philosopher Immanuel Kant (1724–1804). Impartiality could only be achieved, according to Kant, by getting the sentiments, passions, and emotions out of ethics altogether. How you *feel* about someone will not, according to Kant, help you do the right thing. Feelings, sentiments, attachments, and emotions are surefire paths to bias, favoritism, partiality, and self-interest. Inspired partly by Newton and partly by the Christian ethic, which elevates the pure selfless motive above all else, Kant argued that *consequences* be damned. The British ethical tradition focused on the consequences of actions, measuring the ethical value of a deed by the amount of happiness it produced. But Kant looked disdainfully at this shopkeeper cost-benefit analysis of morality and claimed that good *intentions* outweighed all other extrinsic considerations.

The way to purify and perfect ourselves as impartial spectators—who can best judge right from wrong—is to make us into better logicians. Sentimentalists like Adam Smith wanted us to cultivate our feelings of compassion (and our imaginations) in order to act well, but Kant introduced a different imperative.

A hypothetical imperative tells us which means are necessary for attaining a given end. If I want to be healthy, I must eat nutritious food. In this example, the end goal is being healthy and the means is nutritious food. Applied to morals, a utilitarian might offer a hypothetical imperative: If I want the greatest happiness for my family, then I should earn income. But Kant argued that hypothetical imperatives cannot tell us which ends we should choose—they can only guide us about means. Moreover, any appeal to our *experience* in order to settle the rightness or wrongness of an act will fail to give us a universal objective morality because each person's experience will be subjectively different. His solution to this quandary is the famous *categorical imperative.*

Kant's categorical imperative states, "Act only according to that maxim whereby you can at the same time will that it should become a universal law without contradiction."[12] To see how this works, let's apply it to a moral question. I'm hungover and thinking about lying to my boss to avoid work—should I do it? According to Kant, I must consider my possible action of lying *as if* it were a universal law, as if everyone lied to their boss to avoid work. Well, that seems bad from an experiential consequential standpoint because then everybody would be manipulating employers and missing work whenever it was convenient, and labor as we know it would founder. But Kant sees an even deeper problem, a damning logical problem.

If we think about it carefully enough, Kant suggests, we cannot even conceive coherently of a universal law of lying when convenient. Language itself only works if it can be relied upon, but lying renders language unreliable and contradicts its essential function. Therefore, Kant concludes that rationality alone (without reference to context or consequence) renders lying unacceptable.[13]

Trying to re-create social ethics on the model of Newtonian physics may seem like an arcane exercise to contemporary readers, but in fact it directly shaped the U.S. Constitution and the formation of our entire culture. Not only were some of our Founding Fathers friends with Enlightenment philosophers like David Hume, but the new ideas of inalienable human rights (equally apportioned with no regard to name or station) became foundational for the fresh American project. Modern fairness and modern hostility to favoritism were born in the attempt to scientifically systematize human interactions.

According to Enlightenment thinkers, the good life, for the individual and the state, is the rational life. But unlike the ancient Greek notions of rational society (e.g., Plato's *Republic*), the modern view of reason is based on Newtonian ideas of exceptionless laws or inflexible rules. Gravity doesn't have exceptions, so why should human law? The law of inertia doesn't discriminate between bodies—it has no double standard—so why should humans do so in their new scientific societies? The rational life is the logically *consistent* life, the mathematical management of impersonal variables according to formal rules. Even Hume, who always tempered logic with commonsense experience, argued that social life was only possible if we adhered to inflexible universal rules. "Public utility requires that property should be regulated by general inflexible rules; and though such rules are adopted as best serve the same end of public utility, it is impossible for them to prevent all particular hardships, or make beneficial consequences result from every individual case."[14] Making exceptions to these rules—for family, friends, favorites—undermines society itself.

Whether we're talking about Kantian categorical imperatives or impartial spectators, the modern starting place of ethical reflection is an abstract disinterested geometric point—hovering over a grid of impartiality.

When you conceptually lay a perspective grid (like the ones Albrecht Dürer used in his drawings) or a Cartesian coordinate map on a society, you can assess the subjects according to a disinterested objective measuring system (each square in the grid is equal), and you can also compare the subjects to each other objectively. The goal is value neutrality.[15]

Recent psychology data confirms that this grid of impartiality still dominates Western liberal notions of morality. Interviews with subjects from different countries and from different U.S. economic and ethnic demographics reveal that well-educated liberal secular Westerners see morality exclusively as the respecting of individual rights. Fairness between autonomous individual agents is the defining feature of our morality (e.g., cheating is perceived more as unfairness to others—disadvantaging competing agents—rather than as a failure of one's own integrity or a disgrace on one's family). The grid has taken such a strong hold on educated Westerners that they do not even recognize other cultural views of morality. For example, other cultures, immigrant groups, and even rural cultures in the United States think of morality as more than fairness and rights. They think of it as relating to loyalty and patriotism, sacred/profane issues of purity, temperance, obedience to authority, and other values.[16]

Going Off the Grid

Now what happens if I adopt this modern *spectator perspective* for some real-life ethical questions? Let's say I own a tavern, and I regularly book musical groups to entertain the patrons. Many good music combos want to play my tavern, because the crowd is big and appreciative and the pay is decent. My brother, whom I love, has a half-baked uninspired quartet that can muddle through some tunes adequately. I hire his band regularly to perform at the tavern (excessively even), not because he's good or he's the most deserving, but because he's my brother. Have I sinned according to the grid of impartiality? Probably. Looking at the scenario as a disinterested spectator would probably lead me to disfavor my brother. But, from an ethics standpoint, my favoritism here seems like small potatoes. Kant would probably chastise me for letting sentiments infect my decision, but most of us would do the same without much hand-wringing.

In an obvious way, of course, I have to violate a strict egalitarian notion of equal opportunity as soon as I insist that whomever I hire to play the gig is actually a musician. This may seem trivial, but it's interesting how quickly the concept of equal opportunity starts to break down when competence is introduced as a criterion. It's not clear when a musician (or any skilled practitioner) has crossed the mysterious line that separates the qualified from the unqualified. Obvious cases of incompetence are clear enough, but most cases are fuzzy, and the ambiguity creates opportunity for favoritism to decide the competing claims. My brother's band is not awful, but they're also not as good as many of the other bands that are now prevented from playing the gig.

Let's push the example a little further now. Let's say my brother is struggling to make ends meet and provide for his family (my nieces and nephews), so in addition to giving his band slots instead of other, better bands, I give his band a little extra pay than I give the other bands that occasionally play my tavern. This is typical petty favoritism. Again, I've already deviated from the egalitarian grid and the disinterested spectator perspective by preferentially hiring my brother. Now, add a classic skim. At the end of the night, when my brother goes to pay the other musicians in the group, he thinks about how his daughter needs braces and he pockets an extra $20 before he splits the remaining wages equally.

Have ethical norms been violated here? Yes, the ethical framework of fairness has certainly been breached, but the example is innocuous enough to illustrate that the breach is probably acceptable to most of us. Why? Many people when presented with such a case will explain their endorsement on the grounds that it's just a tiny infraction after all and everybody does it anyway—so what's the big deal? This shows, I suspect, that our thinking about such cases is dominated by an official allegiance to fairness, but a cringing willingness to look the other way on minor infractions. It's hard for us to articulate how this violation of the grid could be anything but tolerable failure. But I want to suggest a different way of thinking about the case—a positive vindication of the actions rather than a begrudging toleration. At the same time that the ethical norms of fairness are being violated, another older ethical norm of loyalty and devotion is being fulfilled. There is not *one* ethical framework here (fairness) and some misdemeanor violation. There are two mutually incompatible ethical frameworks here: fairness to all relevant musicians and dedication to kin. You may protest, as Kant might have, that there is only one right thing to do here, but your love of your brother has understandably clouded your ethical judgment (and maybe your failure is even forgivable). But I submit that there are actually two right things to do here, and they intrinsically conflict with each other. Success as an egalitarian citizen is failure as a brother, and vice versa.

Consider some recent well-known cases of nepotism. It is quite likely that filmmaker Francis Ford Coppola opened many doors for some of his family. He didn't just represent *cosa nostra* on film; he practiced its benign nepotism in life. Actors Nicolas Cage and Jason Schwartzman are Coppola's nephews (true *nepotes*), and director Sofia Coppola is Francis Ford Coppola's daughter. Hollywood, like politics, is filled with stories of favoritism. Powerful people frequently smooth the way for their kin in the same ways we all do, but their celebrity status makes the favoritism more public and obvious. Consider, for example, that Sigourney Weaver's dad was the head of NBC, and Jeff Bridges and Beau Bridges benefited from their dad Lloyd Bridges's connections, and Mamie Gummer is a successful New York stage actor and daughter of Meryl Streep, and Will Smith and Jada Pinkett Smith's kids look destined for successful Hollywood careers as well. Let's not forget Martin Sheen's kids, Charlie and Emilio, or Donald Sutherland's son, Kiefer, or Jon Voight's daughter, Angelina Jolie, or Goldie Hawn's daughter, Kate Hudson, or that one guy's daughter Miley Cyrus.

Not many of us are morally outraged by these Hollywood violations of the impartial grid. Like my example of the tavern owner and musicians, these Hollywood cases seem less serious. The social stakes don't seem very high in cases of entertainment favoritism. We tend to write off the whole Hollywood world as play. But of course jobs are jobs, and the money stakes are not trivial in Tinseltown. If preferential hiring automatically discriminates against competing actors, then the grid is violated here too.

Adjust the example a little, and notice a big change in your intuitions. Let's say that I'm not a tavern owner or actor but a Chicago alderman on the city council.[17] I am helping my district build a new youth center, and my brother owns a construction company. I use my influence to help him get the competitive building contract. There are many similarities with the musician example but also important differences. Most people will try to draw a clear line between the private world of the tavern owner and the public world of the alderman. We might be willing to look the other way for the tavern owner's private nepotism, but a public servant who does the exact same thing is usually considered morally reprehensible. The difference seems to be that a public official has accepted a unique role, moving from mere citizen to some kind of administrator or manager of the grid. The egalitarian grid must be upheld in order to ensure equal opportunities in a pluralistic society, but the upholder, in this case, is now required to be *less* of a brother. This fact is frequently ignored or drowned out by the indignant cries of corruption. The alderman's preferential favoritism is said to be a violation of the public trust, but people rarely notice that the alderman's dedication to the grid is a violation of his brotherly duties. Our expectation is that a public official must serve strangers better than his own kin—which is a paradoxical expectation if it's impossible for most people (non-saints) to do this.[18]

My point here is not to defend corrupt aldermen, but to show that the ethics is more complicated than we usually admit. A distinction between public and private duties does not really help us if we realize that tavern owners, actors, aldermen, and all human beings are intermixed amalgams of public and private values, duties and interests. Separating these dimensions from each other and from the person in whom they are hopelessly blended is an artificial head game. Outrage over favoritism is easily sustainable if we adopt the *grid* as our frame of ethics and ignore the special duties of filial ethics. But we do this at a cost. And, interestingly, it's hard to see where all the outrage and indignation is coming from, if the impartial spectator perspective is so disinterested and detached. Perhaps the demand for fairness has a more hidden emotional spring inside it. French political philosopher Alexis de Tocqueville, for example, thought that American principles of equality were heavily motivated by *envy*. We'll examine this more later.

Friendship and Favoritism

Now, what if an alderman gives a contract to a friend? Or a friend of a friend? Not too long ago, at a social event, I raised this question to a group of acquaintances. One of our company grew outraged—practically apoplexic—and he sneered in disgust at what he called the "hopeless corruption of politicians." Shortly after his show of indignation, one of his friends gently reminded him that he got his current job when a mutual friend in management simply appointed him—without any proper job search. He grimaced, stammered something about a previous engagement, and abruptly broke off from our conversation.

Aristotle said, "Without friends no one would choose to live."[19] In the previous chapter, we looked at the development of our *first* favorites, our primordial family clan. We examined how humans and other mammals first establish preferential bonds between parent and offspring. Very early on, however, we begin to admit others into our *circle of favors*. We form non-blood friendships. Our team gets bigger.

Prior to the construction of what I've been calling the great "grid of impartiality," nepotistic friendships were the way that people advanced and even survived in societies. Your family and friendship connections helped you get access to resources, smoothed your path to success, provided you with a loyal and supportive micro community, and made demands on your own wealth and loyalty. Ideologies of political and ethical egalitarianism looked to curtail this nepotistic reality, on the grounds that some groups were "losers" in such a society of favoritism. If you weren't born into the right family or didn't have the right friends, then you remained at a permanent disadvantage.

Constructed in part by Enlightenment philosophy (human rights), in part by legal innovations (e.g., the Napoleonic civil code, common law in Britain and the United States, etc.), and in part by economic transformation (mercantilism and capitalism), the grid did much to alleviate the condition of the underprivileged. And philosopher Montesquieu (1689–1755) claimed early on that *commerce* softens human relations—making us all kinder and gentler—because commerce forces us out of our tribal groups and helps us feel compassion for other social groups. Trading and doing business with strangers begins to reveal their common humanity and elicits sympathy and compassion instead of xenophobia. I'm not sure history bears out this cheerful view of commerce and compassion. Alexis de Tocqueville suggested instead that it was political democracy (not trade) that civilized our social interactions. When we take these things together—Newtonian science, commerce, democracy, social philosophy, and revolutionary ideas of freedom—we arrive at a strange combination of Romantic individualism and classless social idealism. The individual is the most important reality, but every individual is morally indistinguishable and interchangeable with every other individual.

Industrialization further solidified the grid, preventing local folk nepotism from functioning well. The rise of modern urban life put new burdens on social cohesion. People of very different backgrounds fractured off from their nuclear families, migrated into massive cities, and worked shoulder to shoulder with strangers. In the early 1800s, only 3 percent of the world's population lived in cities, but now the figure is estimated to be around 50 percent. Congestion grows rapidly in the post-Enlightenment era and feeds the need for expanded government. If I'm proximally close enough to help you, I'm also close enough to harm you. Without some ideology of fairness, it's hard to imagine this human mayhem working.

Fairness is the management system for large-scale public interactions between strangers, but friendships compromise the system at every turn. The friend always gets and gives special treatment.[20] The friend does not fit squarely in the consistent and regulated grid of impartiality—he looms large in the symbolic picture frame, like a medieval pope towering over tiny commoners.

The friend is not fungible. In the impartial grid, everyone has equal value, and utilitarian divisions of labor entail the interchangeability of anyone who can satisfy the requisite functions. This is the *alienating* feature of modern life, well decried by Karl Marx in the realm of labor and by Franz Kafka in the realm of everything else. But a friend is not interchangeable with another person who has similar skills, talents, or tendencies. Favorites, like friends, are not cogs in the machine. It's true that some people look to "trade up" when someone better comes along, but we generally consider this a shallow betrayal of the real meaning of friendship.

There are no *universal rules* of friendship, no clear rational justifications, no science of friendship. Trying to justify friendships by using

Newtonian-inspired grids of rationality is a fool's errand. My friend is an *exception* to the rules. I can never start with an impartial spectator view of social relations and then arrive at a justification for my friendships—unless I artificially reduce friends to expedient utilitarian resources (i.e., unless I'm a shallow jerk). I cannot find my friend in the hedonic calculus, in the categorical imperative, or even in the legal system. It's not logic or calculation that explains a friendship, but *history*.

It is common for people to describe, excuse, or defend some preferential or exceptional treatment of a friend by shrugging and giving the classic "Well, we have history" answer. That doesn't seem like much of an explanation at first blush, but we grasp the meaning. Sharing experiences with someone, good times and bad, creates a new kind of relationship between people. Biology can bond people together, but so can history—so can shared habits, emotions, and values, as we respond to life events. In a very important sense, I share my life with my friend in a way that I cannot with a stranger. Our shared life is our history. And that unique, contingent history prevents any transferability of friendship. You can't have *substitute* friends.

The non-transferability of friendships becomes obvious when we reflect on the common problem of embarrassing friends. This is more pronounced in politicians and public figures who have more to worry about, but of course we also have that one friend that we just can't take anywhere. As we discussed earlier in the case of the alderman and his brother, politicians are held to a different standard. And in the same way that the alderman is expected to devalue his brotherly duties if they conflict with the public good, so, too, the politician is expected to devalue his friend if there is conflict with the public interest. Sadly, politicians are expected to vouch for the characters of their friends, and God forbid if a politician should be seen with a morally dubious friend.

Some politicians are devoted enough to a friend that they'll hold on to them even as a public media swell condemns the association. This shows how real friendship *history* can trump other considerations— including the threat of political failure or even the temptation to accessorize oneself with more glamorous sycophants, flatterers, and ersatz friends. Unfortunately, many public figures do abandon friends easily, because they can be real liabilities in the political world of pretended saintliness.

When Barack Obama's friend and pastor Jeremiah Wright sermonized a variety of embarrassing and seemingly anti-American views, candidate Obama tried to weather the media storm. But as Wright continued, in 2008, to suggest vaguely racist theories and divisive generalizations (e.g., his weird keynote address to the Detroit branch of the NAACP), Obama decisively broke with Wright and formally left Wright's Trinity United Church of Christ. Presumably, Obama decided that the liability had grown too great. But this was merely an extreme case—accentuated by high-stakes, feverish media attention; most other public figures wrestle more quietly with the demands of friendship and civic duty.

We, the public, expect our civic leaders to have the preposterous fairness of Gandhi, and this unrealistic expectation helps create several problems. First, we're crestfallen if we discover nepotism. Second, public servants must live schizophrenic double lives, because they're not allowed to have normal biases. And third, it encourages the civic success of a whole population of detached, expedient eunuchs, because those are the kind of people who don't take risks or have awkward attachments.

Reasonable Favoritism

When philosophers tried to make ethics into geometry or physics, they did so from the best intentions (i.e., objectivity, they thought, reduces squabbles). But they made a terrible error in thinking that mathematical rationality was the only true reasonable approach to problems.[21] Subjective experiences, biases, personal histories, emotions, and even friendship and kin ties were not compliant in a grid of universal binding rules. My brother, my mom, and my son are not variables in a hedonic calculus or coordinates on a Cartesian lattice. But does this mean that favoritism is intrinsically irrational? No, favoritism is only problematic if we've adopted *theoretical reason* as our paradigm; however, *practical reason* is more capacious and capable of handling the realities of our preferences.[22]

Practical reason is the true foundation for ethics, because it does not pursue theoretical mathematical certainty, but probable, fallible, and context-dependent problem solving. Newtonian-inspired fairness tries to make all people commutative and quickly becomes incoherent when real-life values like favoritism crash the grid. Kant saw all persons as idealized equals, guided by logical consistency. And the utilitarians saw pleasure itself as the commutative and transposable element or variable in the system. But Aristotle starts from *real life* and acknowledges that people are already in a value hierarchy—and the *good* (rather than pleasure) comes in many qualitatively distinct forms.

On friendship, Aristotle starts from some important inequalities.[23] Parents, he explains, are responsible for their children—responsible for their existence, their nurture and upbringing. He considers this to be a case of positive unequal friendship and thinks there are many forms of friendship (e.g., teachers and students, etc.) that imply the "superiority of one party over the other." Now, this talk of superiority rings strange to our egalitarian ear, but his general point is not very controversial. "The justice," he continues, "that exists between persons so related is not the same on both sides, but is in every case apportioned" to merit, to excellence, to usefulness, and to bonds (emotional and blood). Justice is not "the same on both sides"—it is not the commutative relation of fairness. We ought, he says, to render *different* things to parents, siblings, friends, benefactors, and pastors.[24]

Modern sensibilities will balk at the implied (and explicit) patriarchy in Aristotle's description of unequal but legitimate powers. But Aristotle is not simple. He acknowledges that while I owe much to my father, I don't owe him preference in absolutely everything. We should render to each person what is appropriate and befitting.

If Aristotle was Euthyphro and his father had committed manslaughter, then I suspect he'd shelter him (out of feeling and duty). But if, like Frank Calabrese Jr., his father (mob boss Frank Calabrese Sr.) was a vile abuser of everyone (including his sons), then Aristotle would probably find it reasonable, fitting, and appropriate to turn evidence against him.[25] There are no inflexible, universal rules in favoritism, but that doesn't make it less ethical or less reasonable.

Finding the right thing to do, when competing claims are on you, is not like geometry, but it *is* like medicine and other practical sciences (e.g., engineering). A good doctor does not diagnose simply by applying universal rules to particular cases, nor does she treat all bodies alike. Clinical knowledge is acquired by taking a case history. Philosopher Stephen Toulmin characterizes some typical questions in a patient's case history: "To what extent is a patient's condition a result of earlier diseases, accidents, or other misadventures? To what extent must we explain it, rather, by the patient's family background, upbringing, and experience in life? And what pointers do we need to attend to, if we are to see just what the patient's problem is, and how it can best be remedied?"[26]

These techniques are concerned with the particulars of the patient. Health, like *the good*, is not an abstraction that exists independently of patients or people—the actual contingent history of the person will explain the condition and perhaps even suggest the medical way forward. Applied science like medicine is a good analogy with ethics, because the more particular detail we get—or the more concrete complexity—the more likely we are to resolve decisions wisely. As Toulmin puts it, "Set against any fully described problem, abstract principles do not measure up."[27]

Remember the fictional nepotism case from earlier. I'm a tavern owner who preferentially hires his brother the musician. Contrary to the egalitarian interpretation of this favoritism as unethical, I argued that brothers also have legitimate ethical claims on each other and we should really understand these cases as tensions between two competing virtues or goods. But now, even if we grant that two goods are competing, we still need to know how to solve these cases when they come along. Should I always give preferential treatment to my brother? The answer is unclear, even for a fan of favoritism like myself. But the resolution will not come from the application of a grid or even a *theory* about favoritism. Aristotle reminds us that "we must not expect more precision than the subject matter admits."[28] Answers, if there are any, will emerge slowly as a consequence of the details of the case. Watch your own ethical convictions shift, for example, as I add new detail to the brother case.

Let's say that I, the tavern owner, hire my brother Ned's mediocre band, rather than other more competent musical groups in town. I even pay Ned's band extra, because Ned needs financial help. Now, let me adjust the case slightly from the earlier one. Let's say I discreetly pay Ned $150 for the gig, but the other three musicians only get $100 each. This looks bad, right? But not if I keep adding details. The other three musicians in the group are all members of wealthy families, and each of them is living sweetly off their trust funds. They only play music as a hobby and don't need the money. Ned, on the other hand, is not just broke—his daughter needs medical attention. Moreover, Ned dragged the heavy PA speakers and amps from his home, and the other musicians made use of this equipment. I don't know if we feel comfortable now saying that Ned *deserves* the extra $50. But we're more inclined to accept the favoritism as reasonable.

However, I can also complicate this new inclination by adding other details. Ned has a cocaine problem, and it's doubtful that his money will make it home to help his daughter, who he regularly neglects while on his drug benders. My goal here is not to get our moral intuitions flip-flopping, but to show how we can navigate the ethics of favoritism without some theoretical algorithm. The details of the case become crucial.

Here's another: In the spring of 2011, the owner of a media company mobilized his organization to buy a smaller television production company. He was accused of overpaying for the acquisition because his daughter was the owner of the purchased company. Is this a reasonable form of nepotism? Is it different than the case of the tavern-owning brother? It probably doesn't raise your dander much, until I add the following details. The father was billionaire Rupert Murdoch, and he was trying to buy his daughter's company, Shine Group, for $675 million—$320 million of which would go to his daughter Elisabeth.

Now, since Murdoch is the head of a public company and has responsibility to his shareholders, it might be argued that his case is incomparable with my private tavern owner nepotism. Yes and no. Yes, Murdoch has been entrusted with other people's investment money, and as such they have claims on him. But he still has to weigh his "fatherhood duties" toward his daughter against his management duties toward non-relations (and even strangers). It's still no contest, given the disproportionate moral gravity of one's child. Public be damned, if one's daughter can profit. That is the legitimate operating principle of favoritism. However, here is a case, I would argue, where a favoritism operating principle breaks down. Murdoch's daughter is so obscenely advantaged and recklessly compensated in this case, that it seems off the map of decency itself.

Adding more contextual details to the case puts it in a different light than our earlier case. The staggering excesses of the wealth involved here really do change the ethical flavor of the nepotism. What's the difference between the two cases? It's not just the difference in monetary amounts, but the meaning of those amounts. There are different stakes in these cases, because the extra $50 actually improves the life (albeit modestly) of Ned the musician and has negligible negative impact on the other parties involved. Whereas, $320 million is absurdly *over* the threshold of an improved life, and the concentration of that much surplus has a substantial negative impact on the other parties involved. Not to mention the fact that Rupert has no need to inflate the bid for his daughter's company, if the accurate bid is more than she can ever spend in a lifetime of Roman-style debauchery.

The modest nepotism of the brothers seems reasonable, touching, and even a little sad. The nepotism of the Murdochs seems troubling by comparison. But, the grid-lovers will protest and accuse me of being inconsistent in my judgment. To which I respond, yes . . . I'm fine with inconsistency here. The two cases of nepotism are not ethically commutable or interchangeable.

Stoic philosopher Seneca (4 BC?–AD 65) emphasized how giving favors is an art, not a science. "The wise man will compare all things with one another; for the very same object becomes greater or smaller, according to the time, the place, and the cause. Often the riches that are spent in profusion upon a palace cannot accomplish as much as a thousand denarii given at the right time. . . . Often the gift is small, but the consequences great."[29]

Making decisions about favors is not easy. The ethical status of preferential treatment is complex, but we're not totally lost without an abstract grid of fairness.[30] We are left to "feel our way" through a dim territory, but at least practical reason gives us room for history, for exceptions, for hierarchies—for favorites.

4

"But, Dad, That's Not Fair!"

"But, Dad, that's not fair! Why does Keaton get to kill zombies, and I can't?"

"Well, because you're too young to kill zombies. Your cousin Keaton is older than you, so that's why he can do it. You'll get nightmares."

"That's sooo not fair!"

"Next year, after your birthday, I'll let you kill zombies."

It's not exactly *Little House on the Prairie*, but this is a real conversation between my seven-year-old son and me. Age ratings on zombie-killing video games are just one of modern life's great injustices, according to my son.

Every parent has heard the F-word, fairness, intoned ad nauseam by their negotiating kids. My own son was an eloquent voice for egalitarianism, even before he could tie his shoes or tell time. Of course, it's not exactly universal equality that he and other kids are lobbying for, but something much more self-interested.

Kids learn early on that an honest declaration of "I'm not getting what I want" holds little persuasion for parents. So they quickly learn to mask their egocentric frustrations with the language of fairness. An appeal to an objective standard of fairness will at least buy some bargaining time for further negotiations. This is not entirely duplicitous on the part of the child, who is often legitimately confused and cannot easily distinguish his private sufferings from larger and more objective social imbalances.

In this chapter I want to consider the development of fairness in children. We've examined the social construction of the broad value grid of impartiality, but now we'll see how the grid is writ small on the hearts and minds of Western kids. I'll consider the kind of nurturing that instills fairness in our children—the kind that helped instill it in us. And like the last chapter—where I tried to celebrate some of the values and exceptions that fall *outside* the grid—here, too, I'll highlight some of the *losses*, or compromised values, in modern childhood education. As we'll discover, the mastery of an official language of fairness is booming in America, but the natural mother tongue of bias is still our original dialect.

We are such masters of lip service to fairness that we frequently believe our own pretenses. I will show that most of what we teach kids about fairness is actually about other ethical customs, important norms like open-minded tolerance and generosity. These have become conflated with fairness in American education and ideology. Moreover, in addition to seeing too much inside the concept of fairness, I will argue that we also see too little—in the sense that we frequently fail to recognize the darker emotional underbelly (envy) inside our outraged cries for fairness.

The Fusion of Feelings and Ideas

Plato suggested that all human beings contain some horrible ingredients—desires and appetites that should not be pursued. Way before Freud, Plato described the "unlawful" pleasures and appetites. "Every one appears to have them," he explains, "but in some persons they are controlled by the laws and by reason, and the better desires prevail over them—either they are wholly banished or they become few and weak; while in the case of others they are stronger, and there are more of them." When asked for clarification, Plato (through his mouthpiece Socrates) describes the bad appetites as those that wake up in our dreams, "when the reasoning and human and ruling power is asleep; then the wild beast within us, gorged with meat or drink, starts up and having shaken off sleep, goes forth to satisfy his desires; and there is no conceivable folly or shame . . . a man may not be ready to commit."[1]

Most of us readily recognize this frightening character in ourselves. If we never actually act on our low impulses, then at least we recognize this cretin in our wish-fulfillment fantasies.

Whether you agree with Plato here, or the more modern version of the Freudian id, it is well agreed that chaining up or at least disciplining these inner beasties is a major function of socialization and education. In fact, that's why the *Republic*—which many people assume to be a political work—is largely concerned with citizen *education*. How do you create good *character*, when so many corrupting influences live inside and outside you?

Rationalists, like Plato, usually suggest that good character (the healthy psyche or soul) comes when a young person's rational faculty finally tames their lower selfish appetites. One of the main jobs of education and culture generally is to help young people master this internal hierarchy. But even rationalists recognize that reason can't do the job alone (it's pretty unpersuasive on its own), and each individual must enlist the help of their *thumos* (emotion or spirited passion). An *idea* alone or a rational calculation cannot inspire an addict to stop his drug of choice, but *feelings* of self-loathing, resolution, fear, or determination can override the negative behavior.

Similarly, you can't just tell a kid about the Kantian categorical imperative (or some other rational system of ethics) and expect him to start sharing and acting selflessly. Emotions are much better triggers for guiding behavior.

When I was being raised as a devout Catholic, I feared the fires of hell, and this certainly helped shape my early morality. As an adult lapsed Catholic, I had to think up something else to scare my son into submission, and thankfully Santa Claus was a perfect carrot and stick.

Ethical kids aren't born; they're made—and with great effort. This is because Hesiod's old saying is true, right from the start of a kid's life. "Vice in abundance is easy to get; the road is smooth and begins beside you, but the gods have put sweat between us and virtue."[2]

Two points are important here. One is that, despite Hesiod's daunting truth, building an ethical kid does not have to start from scratch. We don't have to import or install feelings into a kid. Nature already gives us the affective head start that I talked about in chapter 2—feelings of empathy and attachment. The job of educating character is to cultivate seed-like ethical feelings into full fruiting sentiments. And the second point to underscore is that ethical feelings and ideologies are already completely mixed and intermingled in the earliest narratives that we tell our kids. Emotions of fear and love, as well as appetites or desires for pleasure or comfort, permeate the early God stories I heard—stories cajoling me to "be a good boy." The same is true of the Santa deceptions that we parents perpetrate on our kids.[3] All this is to say that kids need to be *motivated* to be good, and in our culture that also means they have to be motivated to be fair.

Our ability to feel the suffering or deprivation of another person is part of our instinctual equipment, and we see rudimentary versions of this sympathy in other primates. It starts as a simple, almost mechanical, *emotional contagion*. Babies often cry, for example, when they perceive another crying baby. Emotions are highly contagious for mammals, and we observe that anger, joy, and fear (among others) can spread rapidly through a group, even when there's no cognitive awareness of what's going on. Mammal bodies can read other mammal bodies.

The recent discovery of "mirror neurons" suggests that our social brains are so sensitive to the feelings and actions of others, that *my* same neural pain pathways light up or activate when I see *you* undergoing some painful experience. I literally feel a little taste of your pain, just by witnessing it. The subjective wince that I feel at your suffering is neurologically underwritten by automatic brain processing.[4]

There is a "shared manifold" of feelings or even an "emotional atmosphere" that humans share with one another. It's not mystical or spooky; it's just an under-recognized perceptual ability. This seems

Fig. 12. Our ability to feel the suffering of another person is part of our instinctual equipment, and we see rudimentary versions of this sympathy in other primates. It starts as a simple, almost mechanical, *emotional contagion*. Babies cry, for example, when they perceive another crying baby. Drawing by Stephen Asma.

crucial for the development of our more sophisticated feelings of empathy and our eventual sense of justice. It's only because I can feel your pain that I can recognize some forms of injustice.

Child psychologist Jean Piaget (1896–1980) didn't know about mirror neurons, but he knew that a child's empathic instincts help her construct moral rules through the social interaction of play.[5] Both Freud and sociologist Émile Durkheim saw children as passive recipients of external moral rules and regulations, but Piaget crawled around on the floor with kids and discovered that they actively shape their own sense of justice—they role-play and take the perspective of others, all the while gauging their relevant empathic feelings. As a child matures, she can feel directly and indirectly (in the course of game play) that some actions hurt and some are pleasurable, and a Golden Rule notion of justice organically emerges. A sense of fairness emerges, according to Piaget, as children engage in cooperative decision making and problem solving. This led him to recommend greater cooperative interpersonal activities in early childhood education.

Kids learn about fairness in their nuclear families by practicing sharing behaviors, and children in larger families probably learn a bit more of it than those in single-child families. We also, however, tell certain kinds of cultural stories and make certain educational moves that try to shape this organic emotional atmosphere. Contemporary stories in books, television shows, songs, movies, and eventually school all converge to inculcate the grid of impartiality.

Sowing the Seeds of Confusion: Sharing

Long-running television shows like *Sesame Street* (forty years), *Mister Roger's Neighborhood* (thirty-one seasons), *The Wonderful World of Disney* (forty-four years, first as *Walt Disney's Wonderful World of Color*), and *Romper Room* (forty-one years) have helped shape a couple generations of young American egalitarians. The future wave of long-running morality plays will probably include *Thomas the Tank Engine and Friends*, *Barney*, and *SpongeBob SquarePants*, among others.

As a kid I consumed a lot of this stuff. As a father, I have ingested several more courses of this diet, and I can say that much of it is absolutely wonderful. I'm not a conservative critic of pop culture. Not only are there smart, intelligent stories, but great life lessons about pride, caring, selfishness, love, anger management, and justice.

Most of the stories of children's culture, however, pull a sleight-of-hand trick on kids and on us. They regularly address two worthy topics that every child should cultivate—namely, *sharing* and *open-mindedness* (toward people who are different). But while we all approve of the great virtues of sharing and multicultural appreciation, we are informed that these are matters of fairness and equality—which, in point of fact, they are not. Sharing what we have is a major theme of all the above kids' television shows, but also a major theme of many fairy tales, fables, and narratives (e.g., *Robin Hood*, *A Christmas Carol*, *Stone Soup*, *How the Grinch Stole Christmas*, *The Giving Tree*, and so on).

Many people think that when they're teaching their kids to not be selfish, they are in fact teaching them fairness. We assume this is true because our culture uses the term "fair" in a sloppy way, to mean anything good or just. But learning to curb selfishness is not the same thing as fairness.

Reducing a child's greediness is not the same as making her egalitarian. One can eliminate greed entirely and still remain preferential with one's goods, one's time, and one's affection. Like the characters in many kids' stories, our children are encouraged to spread the wealth, whether it be money, magic beans, or candy.

Greed is a terrible vice, and generosity must be cultivated in order to counteract it—but a child should not be expected to distribute her wealth to just anyone on the playground. And even if she has enough candy for the whole playground population, each playground kid does not have a moral claim on her to receive some candy. A child might be so generous, in fact, that she gives away all her candy and does not even retain some for herself. But the quality of her generosity—the strength of her virtue—is not compromised by the fact that she gave it all to her five friends. She is still a very generous kid. A person might give everything she has, in fact, to one other person and thereby show profound generosity. And this demonstrates the independence of generosity (or sharing) from fairness, even though the two are often conflated in our cultural conversation. A person can be both highly generous and highly biased at the same time. Being in favor of favoritism, then, is not being against sharing.

Most kids first encounter talk of fairness while engaging in sandbox politics. Such play involves sharing toys and playing games (taking turns in who picks the game, how it is played, and so on). "Fairness" is the catchall term that usually gets applied to these diverse norms. And in some cases, it's accurate. For example, taking turns at being "it" in tag or the seeker in hide-and-seek is an issue of how an inferior or superior position is equally distributed. But parents also misapply the term (and kids adopt it) to other sorts of ethical norms—norms that have nothing to do with equality. For example, sandbox politics asks kids to respect one another's feelings and property, to share things, to compromise on conflicting matters, to learn how to defer to "experts"

Fig. 13. Most kids learn the language of fairness in the course of (parent-guided) sandbox politics and peer interaction. But "fairness" doesn't begin to cover the real normative complexities of the social territory that kids find themselves in. Drawing by Stephen Asma.

(e.g., kids to adults, kindergartners to first-graders, etc.), and generally to learn how to discipline and modulate oneself in the uneven context of other agents.

However, equal distribution of power and goods—even in sandbox politics—is quite rare and, more importantly, beside the point. Some kids have amazing plastic trucks, some kids are charismatic and dominate games, some kids are familiar play pals while others are new to the sandbox, and some frighten the whole group with dog-deafening screams and tantrums. The whole thing is a hierarchic, biased, imbalanced mess—but it works. It's not really an exercise in fairness, and yet we tend to use this terminology in our attempts to moralize and guide the chaos.

Our official language of fair play rides on top of the actual complexities of childhood values as a comically simple veneer. And even a closer look at the culture of children's stories and programs reveals a more subtle and rich set of value representations. We *say* we're all about the fairness, but our more enduring stories dive into deeper waters.

The wildly popular Pixar/Disney franchise *Toy Story*, for example, reveals more depth about favoritism than most "official" ethical instructions to kids. The "emotional atmosphere" of the well-known trilogy of films is a boy who loves his toys, but some more than others. There is tension and humor because Woody, the favorite toy, feels threatened by a new contender for favorite status (in this case, Buzz Lightyear), but the value inequalities are recognizable and relatable to every kid who sees it. Thankfully, the film does not offer a disingenuous denouement in which the boy learns to love and treat all his toys equally. Instead, we find a mature ethical universe depicted, where the toys recognize their relative places in the boy's heart—and in one another's—and flourish just fine within the hierarchical realities of favoritism. My suspicion is that such Disney stories and many fairy tales, for that matter, work so well on us because they speak more directly to our *limbic* values, rather than our official socially authorized values.[6]

Many folk tales, fairy tales, and contemporary kids' stories reveal and even lionize favoritism, without ever admitting it. *The Velveteen Rabbit* (1922) and many similar-themed stories, for example, convey the idea that loving something or someone intensely enough can actually change the beloved's metaphysical status. Favoritism can even transform an inanimate toy into a living creature. Or consider further the positive depictions of Christopher Robin and his favorite Winnie-the-Pooh. And *The Lion King* is not only about the favorite son of the savanna, Simba, but it is also rife with unapologetic social hierarchies that run exactly counter to most egalitarian values. To my mind, these stories are good and their popularity stems from their honest engagement with our unegalitarian limbic systems of favoritism. The stories speak truths that are not acceptable or discussable in the official grid of impartiality.

Sowing the Seeds of Confusion: Open Minds

Teaching kids to *share* and calling it *fairness* is at best a confusion and at worst a deception. A similar bait-and-switch in contemporary childhood education is teaching kids to appreciate diversity but erroneously calling this virtue of open-mindedness "fairness." These two different values are so commonly confused with one another that any critique is immediately met with charges of prejudice, discrimination, racism, sexism, and bigotry. But I wish to suggest that having favorites and having an open mind about differences are not mutually exclusive.

Lesson plans for elementary teachers are great windows into a culture's value system. Studying educational guidelines and lesson literature in the United States and abroad reveals a mishmash of ethics-based learning objectives. A recent Texas elementary school curriculum document, called "Justice and Fairness," is highly indicative. The teacher is advised to introduce the topic to students by first defining terms. "Justice" we are told is "treating everyone fairly under established rules and laws." Equating "justice" and "fairness" is a pervasive muddle in education, but then things get murkier as "fairness" is used to mean the sum total of disconnected virtues: "treating all people with honesty and respect," "cooperating with one another," "giving everyone equal opportunities to succeed," "making sure others are not treated badly," and also "celebrating the uniqueness and value of everyone."

Students are taken through a series of exercises that reinforce the idea that "being fair" is the same thing as "being good." Teachers of all elementary grades are told to display an egg and a glass of water to the children. Placing the egg inside the glass, the teacher tells the students (as it sinks to the bottom) that this egg is like a person "who is not being treated fairly." The egg "represents how someone who is left out or mistreated would feel—sad, depressed, defeated, unappreciated, and unloved." Now the teacher should remove the egg and add salt to the water, equating the salt with "honesty and respect." Next, the teacher should draw a smiley face on the egg and return it to the water glass. The egg will now float. The teacher should explain that the egg is now "being supported with kindness and 'held up' by the fairness and acceptance of others."[7] Students are then introduced to the pantheon of fairness fighters: Martin Luther King Jr., Rosa Parks, Abraham Lincoln, and Susan B. Anthony.

It's daunting to launch a critique on this, when I am myself a moderate liberal and a dedicated devotee of the above pantheon. But my critique seeks to preserve these virtues and these heroes, while dispatching the hypocrisy of calling it all "fairness." It's not just bad speaking, but bad thinking to conflate all this stuff. Respecting diverse people is an obvious good, but it does not require or entail that I lay aside my own favoritism.

I share the belief that xenophobia is ever looming and needs constant correction and prevention at the elementary-school level. The challenges of today's globalization are really just continuations of those historical tests of pluralism in melting-pot American. A massive 2004 European training manual for teachers, called *Diversity and Equity in Early Childhood Training in Europe*, makes it clear that Europe is trying to combat the social exclusion of immigrant groups and strengthen pluralistic inclusion.[8] European and United States education systems are valiantly and justifiably simmering their respective melting pots to ensure fewer boil-overs.

The *Diversity and Equity* manual invites teachers and students to engage in a variety of exercises designed to give greater awareness and perspective on the inequalities of minority life. In an Irish workshop called "The Dominant Walk," for example, teachers are asked to "walk a mile in the shoes" of different people. Each Irish teacher is given a "profile" of a child living in contemporary Ireland (e.g., a white Irish five-year-old with an elder brother in boarding school, or a black four-year-old Dubliner boy who is deaf, or a four-year-old Traveller girl living at a nomadic site, and so on). Then the teacher must walk around, adopting the profiled child's identity, and "consume" the cultural images of race, gender, and class that abound in everyday magazines, billboards, television, newspapers, and so on. According to the manual, teachers learn how underrepresented groups fail to show up in the imagery of dominant culture (i.e., they're invisible) or show up exclusively as "problems" (e.g., as criminals, poor, etc.). From this lesson, they are encouraged to wallpaper their own classroom environments with more inclusive imagery—representations of minorities that lead children to feel like they belong.

This whole exercise seems like a wonderful way to sensitize teachers and students to subtle forms of discriminatory cultural exclusion. I have no complaint with its purpose or its execution, but here's the rub. The *Diversity and Equity* manual, just like American schools, equates open-mindedness with fairness throughout its many exercises, and sees all tribal tendencies as the enemy. Favoritism and bias are demonized and treated as equivalent to bigotry. For example, the manual recommends exercises for kids using an "Anti-bias Persona Doll." The Anti-bias Persona Doll started in the United States but has also been embraced in European diversity training. The method uses dolls of various ethnic appearances to tell stories of mistreatment. Kids are asked to help rectify scenarios wherein the persona has suffered some prejudice and mistreatment. So far so good, but children are taught that all bias is unfair and that fairness *is* equity, which is only possible after bias has been eradicated. Teachers join in this fight against favoritism and bias—the manual claims that the best way to fight against the evils of racism, sexism, and social power imbalance is to use what they call the "anti-bias" approach. Teachers are taught, in workshops, to find their own biases (in a therapeutic session) and then root them out—to cleanse themselves of any subjective hierarchic evaluations of students and colleagues. The manual states that we should find our idiosyncratic ways of "othering the other" and purify ourselves of these tendencies.

I want to argue something radical here. Contrary to all this received wisdom, I want to suggest that open-mindedness is actually compatible with favoritism and bias.

Recent child psychologists, focusing on group attitudes and relations, have discovered a more nuanced picture than the received wisdom of the last fifty years. In 1954 the Supreme Court cited a 1947 study (by Kenneth B. Clark and Mamie Phipps Clark) in their landmark *Brown v. Board of Education* case. The "doll test" study showed that black children in segregated schools preferred white dolls to black dolls, and the investigators argued that this showed a loss of self-esteem resulting from the segregated school environment.

Starting in the 1950s, researchers, inspired by this important study, began running children through a variety of racial preference play tests and "trait assignment" tasks. The Preschool Racial Attitude Measure II (1975) and the Multiple-Response Racial Attitude measure (1988) asked kids to assign positive and negative traits to images of black and white children. Researchers wanted to see if kids assign traits, like "nice" or "mean" or "dirty" or "clean," based solely on racial features. Since some of this trait assignment does correlate with racial differences, it was thought to be evidence for early childhood racism. Kids seem to be negative and prejudiced toward *out-groups*—toward groups of different racial or ethnic or cultural background. This view fits with a long-held bit of folk wisdom: people come together against a common enemy or set of strangers. Racial differences seem to create solidarity out of negativity. And the "narcissism of minor differences" will lead in-groups and out-groups to form over more trivial differences than race. This view has mixed with developmental theories, like Piaget's, and become part of a story that describes all kids as moving from early childhood *selfishness*, to intermediate *group concern*, to the final stage of principled *fairness* for all. Each predecessor is considered an impediment to its successor.

More recent research, however, has shown something very interesting, something counter to all this folk wisdom.[9] Yes, in-group bias is very strong —we identify with people who most resemble us—but it doesn't really correspond with *negativity* toward out-groups in the way we previously thought. The earlier testing (trait-assignment tasks) forced kids into false dichotomies. Given only a narrow set of positive and negative traits and racial subjects to designate, kids automatically preferred their own similar in-groups, and then had no other choice but to assign negative traits to those individuals and groups who were different. More subtle testing shows that group favoritism does not automatically entail negative judgments or attitudes toward out-groups. Without the forced dichotomy testing, kids will report neutral traits and other positive traits to out-groups, not just negative traits.[10]

These more recent findings undermine the old assumption that favoritism automatically entails bigotry toward out-groups. Intergroup relationships and judgments, even among kids, are much more complex than we thought. Kids *simultaneously* make social evaluations based on at least three different criteria: self-interests, group interests, and justice interests.[11] The old folk wisdom that group closeness comes from negative opposition to others is not borne out by recent data. Nor is the old developmental story that we all start out as egotistical Hobbesians who slowly learn to care for others. This last point ties in with my earlier argument in chapter 2 that our biological default interests are family (tribal) oriented *before* they are egoistically oriented. Psychologists now suggest, "Instead of characterizing moral development as a series of hierarchical stages beginning with a selfish focus that transforms into group concerns and culminates in a justice principle, social domain researchers have demonstrated that people weigh personal, group and fairness principles simultaneously when making decisions about the right thing to do."[12]

In short, favoritism or bias toward your group is not intrinsically racist, sexist, or closed-minded. Privileging your tribe does not render you negative or bigoted toward those outside your tribe. And to top it off, we're now beginning to understand the flexible nature of our in-group favoritism—it doesn't have to carve up along bloodlines, race lines, or ethnic lines. Psychological experiments reveal a whole range of criteria for in-group bias.[13] For example, test subjects have been shown to award higher payoffs to arbitrary in-groups, like people who just happen to share the same birthday as the test subject. And in-group bias can be demonstrably strong when subjects share allegiance to the same sports teams, and so on.

Young people in our schools are repeatedly exposed to a bogus association between "unbiased equality for all" and "open-mindedness." But even with the laudable pantheon of fairness fighters, paraded before elementary students, each has an origin in in-group favoritism. Rosa Parks and Susan B. Anthony were not fighting for the equality of all people per se, but for the inclusion of their in-groups. It's no disservice to them or denigration of them to point out this basic fact of favoritism. Some serious allegiance to one's tribe is, after all, how anything gets done at the social level—including civil rights.

Cicero, in his essay on friendship, praised favoritism in a way that celebrates its positive aspects without accepting or acknowledging it (as moderns do) as some impediment to liberal tolerance:

> For it seems clear to me that we were so created that between us all there exists a certain tie which strengthens with our proximity to each other. Therefore, fellow countrymen are preferred to foreigners and relatives to strangers, for with them Nature herself engenders friendship. . . . Moreover, how great the power of friendship is may most clearly be recognized from the fact that, in comparison with the infinite ties uniting the human race and fashioned by Nature herself, this thing called friendship has been so narrowed that the bonds of affection always unite two persons, or at most, a few.[14]

Envy and Fairness

When a young child complains that something is unfair, it is often easy to see the envy lurking beneath the thin veil of moral indignation. Adults are slyer in disguising their feelings as piety, but they frequently have little more justification than the child. Philosopher Friedrich Nietzsche (1844–1900) was an acute observer of human subterfuge and noticed that some of the most righteous pious people are some of the most angry, lustful, and vengeful people you'll ever meet. He famously dissected the virtue of chastity, for example, to reveal lustful sensuality seething—frustrated—just below the surface.[15] Is there a similar psychodynamic in our indignant demands for fairness? Do we detect some bitterness and resentment skulking under our high-toned demands for fairness?

Many kids and even adults see fairness in punitive terms. Lofty egalitarian philosophy about a utopian grid of equality is noble when legislators are framing constitutions, but the rest of us usually cry "unfair" when we feel slighted, snubbed, or envious of others. Feeling injured, as an individual or group, is strong fuel for our obsession with fairness.

Alexis de Tocqueville (1805–1859), the French philosopher and historian, studied America and pronounced, "Equality is a slogan based

Fig. 14. The biblical story of Cain and Abel reveals a preferential God and also gives us an early glimpse into the madness of envy. Here God smiles on Abel's blood sacrifice and frowns on Cain's grain approach. Drawing by Stephen Asma, based on medieval representations.

on envy. It signifies in the heart of every [American] 'Nobody is going to occupy a place higher than I.' "[16] More than an American problem, of course, envy seems built into the human condition. Social utopians suggest that vices like envy and jealousy are contingent upon political economy, and if we just got rid of private property, we'd have no cause to envy others. On the other hand, the story of Cain and Abel as well as the work of ancient Greek tragedians suggest that envy didn't need to wait for capitalism to goad the hearts of men.

Envy is considered a sin in Christianity and a terrible addiction in Buddhism, but it has an upside too. It can energize and motivate a person to strive harder for what they want. In the Buddhist *Bhikkhuni Sutta* (*Anguttara IV*), the monk Ananda—the Buddha's right-hand man—avoids the righteous talk and admits that sometimes a transgression is the best way to kick-start a virtue. He says that sometimes conceit is the way to overcome conceit. For example, a young traveler on the dharma path may see the freedom and equanimity of a more experienced monk and say to himself, "I'm better than him, and if he can do it, so can I." And so an immature feeling may lead, like a catalyst, to greater effort, resolve, and the real attainment of inner peace. Perhaps similarly immature feelings of envy can evolve into more noble efforts to fairly redistribute wealth or goods or influence. Regardless of this issue, it seems clear that fairness has a painful emotional feeling creeping inside it—the grieving feeling of wanting what my neighbor has.

What does my neighbor have? He has reputation, and I do not. He has wealth, and I do not. He has interesting friends, he has opportunity, he has a better wife, better kids, better morals, better fashion sense, better piano skills, a better diploma, a bigger penis. Envy knows no bounds and can thrive in the ghetto or the country club.

Theologians and philosophers have labored to unpack the nuances of envy and have noticed that we tend to envy those who are closer to our own lifestyle and class. Thomas Aquinas (1225–1274) writes, in his *Summa Theologica*, that "a man does not strive for mastery in matters where he is deficient; so that he does not envy one who surpasses him in such matters, unless he surpass him by a little, for then it seems to him that this is not beyond him."[17] I, for one, confess that I envy my neighbor's big backyard more than the wealth of Bill Gates, whose net worth seems more remote, fantastical, and even preposterous. Aquinas also cites Aristotle, who commented that the elderly envy the young for their health and beauty, and nearly everyone hates to see another person gain with ease what you yourself acquired through sweat and difficulty. I have been heard to utter, "It's not fair," for example, when I contemplate that my neighbor doesn't work any harder than me, and yet he flourishes in his obscene estate of a backyard—he and his enormous lawn mocking me. Okay, let's move on.

Finally, Aquinas sums up, "We grieve over a man's good, in so far as his good surpasses ours; this is envy properly speaking, and is always sinful, as also the Philosopher (Aristotle) states, because to do so is to grieve over what should make us rejoice, viz. over our neighbor's good."

I don't share Aquinas's characterization of envy as a "sin," but I agree that it's not one of our better human traits. If envy burns naturally in the human breast, then some cultural trends seem to fan the flames more than others. For example, children and parents were taught something very different about envy in the nineteenth century than in our current culture.[18] Parents taught their children to accommodate negative feelings like envy by using Stoic resolve. When educational philosopher Felix Adler analyzed the biblical Cain and Abel parable, in his 1892 *The Moral Instruction of Children*, he exhorted young people to master and suppress their feelings of envy or else they would end up like murderous Cain (recall that envy led Cain to kill his brother Abel after God preferentially favored Abel's animal sacrifice). Envy was to be treated with self-discipline. There will always be people better off than you, and the sooner you accept and conquer your envy, the better off you'll be.

Historian Susan J. Matt argues that all this changed in the twentieth century, and by the 1930s a whole new childhood education regarding envy was in full swing. Social workers "praised parents who bought extra gifts for their children. If a son or daughter needed a hat, adults should buy it, but they should also purchase hats for their other offspring, whether or not they needed them. This would prevent children from envying one another."[19]

The phenomenon of *sibling rivalry* had made it into the textbooks as a potentially damaging pattern of envy—one that is best addressed by giving all the kids an equal fair share of everything. Subduing or restraining one's feelings of deprivation and envy was considered "old school," and new parents (living in a more prosperous nation) sought to stave off these feelings in their children by giving them more stuff.

This trend—of assuaging feelings of deprivation by distributing equal goods to children—grew even stronger in the baby boom era and beyond. It has also dovetailed nicely with the rise of an American consumer culture that defines the good life in part by material acquisition.[20] Today's culture tries to spare kids the pains of sibling and peer rivalry, but does so by teaching them directly and indirectly to channel their envy into the language and expectation of fairness—and a reallocation of goods that promises to redress their emotional wounds.

If our high-minded notions of retributive justice have roots in the lower emotions of revenge, then why should we be surprised if fairness has roots in envy?[21] I have no illusions and feel entirely comfortable with the idea that fairness has origins in baser emotions like envy. But most egalitarians will find this repugnant and damaging to their saintly and selfless version of fairness. For my part, I draw a comparison between some of the indignant, angry demands for fairness and those hypocritical priests who denounce the evils of sensuality but take their own illicit pleasures in private. "I have always observed a singular accord between supercelestial ideas and subterranean behavior," Montaigne reminds us.[22]

Secular calls for fairness can frequently resemble, in emotional tone and language, the older religious calls for piety. Emotions of guilt, envy, and indignation energize religions, but in a post-religious era those emotions just find new secular outlets. The same demographic for whom religion has little or no hold (namely, white liberals) turns out to be the most virulent champions of all things fair. Is it possible that these folks must vent their moral spleen on egalitarian causes because they don't have all the theological campaigns (e.g., opposing gay marriage, opposing abortion, etc.) on which social conservatives exercise their indignation? Don't get me wrong, I think the liberal venting is healthier than the conservative, but I'm trying to expose the rarely acknowledged emotional core of the supposedly cool-headed principled egalitarian.[23]

Psychologist Jonathan Haidt and Craig Joseph found that elite white college-educated people are the only demographic that see morality as primarily a matter of fairness. For this demographic, justice is a contractual affair that fairly distributes goods and protects rights.[24] This population tends to think of ethics in cost-benefit terms. Other demographics, both inside and outside the United States, have different emotional foundations for morality. The differences are often matters of degree and weighting, but it's clear that some cultures stress *compassion* over fairness/reciprocity, or they stress *loyalty* over fairness, or *authority*, or issues of moral *purity*.

I'm suggesting that envy plays a significant role as one of the building blocks of fairness morality. Social psychologist Jan-Willem van Prooijen argues that "fairness judgments are mostly based on how people feel about a situation: People intuitively feel good or bad about a situation, and based on this moral sentiment, people conclude whether or not a given situation is fair or unfair." Van Prooijen suggests that most of us start our assessment of a moral issue from an egocentric perspective, and "it follows that people's fairness judgments are based on the extent to which people experience a particular situation as good or bad for themselves."[25] If a person feels no *envy* when they encounter a specific scenario, they are unlikely to perceive it or label it as unfair. But somehow this important subjective ingredient is invisible to us when we reflect on (and implement) our moral convictions.[26]

It may be important to remind ourselves that the framers of the Declaration of Independence almost adopted John Locke's three human rights: life, liberty, and *property*. When it came to our Declaration, Jefferson altered the precursor document (the Virginia Declaration of Rights) to read "happiness" instead of property—but everyone saw property as crucial. A political economy based on private property may not automatically engender a culture of envy, but I'm pretty sure that *consumer* ideology (emerging in the twentieth century) does. Fairness morality fits well with an idea of the good life that is bound up with consumption. This is because fairness (as a measurement) applies exceedingly well to quantifiable things like property and material goods. Morality as "distribution of wealth" turns the lens away from other moral issues like character, loyalty, and integrity, and focuses instead on equity and parity. We shouldn't overstate the importance of this correlation, however, since envy also provides emotional underpinning for *honor-based* cultures too.

Excellence, Fairness, and Favoritism

"Honor" is not a word you'll hear very often in contemporary America. You might hear it in military families and military culture, but elsewhere it only seems to crop up ironically. Honor used to be wed to the idea of merit and excellence, but it has slipped from ordinary language. The words "merit" and "excellence" are holding on for dear life, but they seem to be slipping too. Their last holdout arena seems to be sports. But notice the divorce between honor and merit in the fact that while many of us love their athletic prowess, we don't consider athletes honorable characters—in fact, they frequently seem spoiled and ignoble.

Egalitarian values and cultures largely replaced Western honor cultures because those earlier ideologies of reputation had created inequities of prestige, goods, and opportunities. But along with the dispatch of honor came great threats to the cultures of excellence and merit. The merit-based critique of fairness is well known. Plato spends much of the *Republic* railing against democracy on the grounds that know-nothing dolts should never have equal political voice with experts (*aristoi*). "Elitism" is a dirty word in our culture, but it was not so for the ancients.

American hostility to elitism was made manifest during the election and presidency of Barack Obama, who repeatedly had to downplay his own intelligence and intellectual accomplishments so that he might seem less threatening (less eggheadish) to the public. It is common for American public figures to apologize for their intelligence, or try to conceal it, in order to win over the public. Bill Clinton, for example, is a highly accomplished intellectual (e.g., Georgetown University, multiple academic fraternity memberships, Rhodes Scholar at Oxford, Yale Law School, etc.), but he downplayed this in his campaign. Clinton defused anti-intellectual hostility by playing up his "regular guy" qualities, winning over many Americans by playing saxophone on the *Arsenio Hall Show* and feasting on junk food.[27]

I am in agreement with many of the merit-based critiques of egalitarian fairness. I don't want my political leaders to be "regular guys." I want them to be elite in knowledge and wisdom. I want them to be exceptional.

As I mentioned in chapter 1, I don't want my son and every other kid to be told they "won" the footrace at school, just because we think their self-esteem can't handle the truth. Other elementary-school policies also foster the dogma of fairness. Sports and games have been modified so that no one scores, or at least the score is not kept or tallied. Also, kids in physical education class are now chosen for teams by random lotteries rather than the old-school method, wherein the captains chose from best to worst athletes. In those days—standing in the schoolyard lineup—all of us could witness the painful truths of our relative athletic excellence. But no one was "broken" by those painful truths. First, changing the game to a different sport frequently reorganized the order of best-to-worst players (it was painful to be last, but exhilarating to be first chosen). Second, learning (in the worst-case scenario) that you really suck at all sports is important information to discover as you claw your way toward some juvenile identity. Praising the tough love of ugly truths, writer James Poniewozik quips that "encouragement helps us reach for the stars; realism prevents us from pursuing a midlife career change as an astronaut."[28]

The contrast of our system with merit-based Chinese preschool is astounding. The goals and assumptions of Chinese education are very different from ours, and some of this will be clearer in the next chapter, but consider one indicative example: the Storytelling King.

Imagine your four-year-old preschooler getting up the nerve to stand in front of her class and tell an elaborate story to her eagerly attentive classmates. It's a sweet rite of passage that many children enjoy around the world, and it builds self-esteem and confidence too. Now, imagine that when your preschooler is finished spinning her yarn, she stands at the front of the classroom while the other children tell her that her story was way too boring. One kid points out that he couldn't understand it, another kid says that her voice was much too quiet, another says that she paused too many times, and another tells her that her story had a terrible ending. In most schools around the world, this scenario would produce a traumatic and tearful episode, but not so in China, where collective criticism is par for the course—even in preschool.

At Daguan elementary school, in Kunming, China, this daily gauntlet is called the Storyteller King.[29] Each kid gets up and tells a story to the whole class, and then fellow students and teachers dissect and critique the student, sometimes with brutal honesty. American teachers who saw this exercise were horrified by it. But it is indicative of Chinese merit-based culture. Similarly, consider that students' test scores and grades are posted publicly in China for all to see. There is no anonymity to the grades—everyone can see their position and that of others in the meritocracy. Contrast this with my own situation as an American college professor. I am not allowed to reveal a student's grade to anyone but the student, as it is considered a violation of the student's privacy. If I publicly posted the merit-earned grades of my students, I could lose my job. And this reveals the radical difference between public morality culture (shame-based) and private morality culture (guilt-based). More importantly, it also reveals egalitarianism at work. Teachers and students in the West must present everyone as equal, even when they demonstrably are not.

The Chinese are not interested in cultivating *individuality* in their kids, but they are devoted to excellence and even *virtuosity*. This seems almost paradoxical to Westerners, who associate virtuosity with individualism. But excellence, as conceived by Confucian cultures, is more about mastery of established levels of refinement, rather than innovation. Chinese education and culture are extremely hierarchical, but this meritocratic system actually produces character modesty, rather than arrogance. It is well known that Chinese students outperform their American counterparts in most academic areas, but lesser known is the fact that they seem to outstrip Americans in modesty and humility.

When psychologists Harold Stevenson and James Stigler compared the academic skills of grade-school students in three Asian nations to U.S. students, the Asian students easily outstripped the American ones. However, when the same students were subsequently asked to rate their academic prowess, the American kids expressed much higher self-appraisals than their Asian counterparts. "In other words," journalist Steve Salerno writes, "U.S. students gave themselves high marks for lousy work. Stevenson and Stigler saw this skew as the fallout from the backwards emphasis in American classrooms; the Brookings Institution 2006 Brown Center Report on Education also found that nations in which families and schools emphasize self-esteem cannot compete academically with cultures where emphasis is on learning, period."[30]

While I am in agreement with many of the merit-based critiques of egalitarian fairness, I must distinguish these critiques from my main point about favoritism. In the same way that egalitarianism is no friend of meritocracy, neither is favoritism. Favoritism and meritocracy are both hierarchical and share an antagonism toward fairness, but in every other sense they are strange bedfellows and antagonize each other too.

Favoritism does indeed create social hierarchies of value, and frequently it does this at the expense of merit and excellence. My favorites are not the best or most accomplished at this or that. They are not virtuoso human beings. It's my sheer affection for them, and my ability to relate to them, that raises their status above other people.

Schools try to level the hierarchy of favoritism. In the same way that parents are desperate to avoid sibling rivalry at home, schools insist on impartiality among the student body. Today's U.S. school kids are discouraged from openly expressing favoritism. As I mentioned in chapter 1, kids are not allowed to bring valentine cards or treats to exchange, unless they bring enough for everyone. I was even told repeatedly by teachers that I could not bring half the class cookies and the other half cupcakes, because even though everyone was provided for, all the students should have the exact same treat.

Favoritism between friends or between teachers and students is assumed to disadvantage the others in the group, but if my previous argument is valid—that in-group favoritism is not the same as out-group discrimination—then favoritism in school need not hinder others. When resources (like instruction time and supplies) are scarce, then of course the distribution must be just, but many forms of favoritism are helpful to education. Favorite teachers motivate students; favorite students inspire teachers; favorite classmates help one another. Mentors who are allowed to choose their protégés are not just discriminating, but carefully judging whether their special knowledge or skills can be safely entrusted to this person. Favorite pupils in this scenario are not only privileged but burdened with greater responsibility. Perhaps the greatest obstacle to these more subtle, affectionate forms of education and edification is just the large numbers of people processed in modern institutions.

One of the major objections to favoritism in an institution like a school is that extra attention leaves some people on the outside of a privileged circle. Fairness is intoned in order to rescue the "outcast." Obviously this pulls on the heartstrings, and I am not arguing that outsiders are acceptable collateral damage in the enactment of favoritism. But I am suggesting that *everyone* is a favorite to *someone*. Being an insider or outsider is relative, not absolute. The only harmful or sad thing is if a person is *never* preferred by anybody—an extremely rare scenario that cannot be fixed by eliminating favoritism, anyway. Most people have rich personal lives, complete with families and friends who see them as beloved favorites. Any ethical responsibility to celebrate their importance and significance falls to their families, friends, and tribes—not strangers, associates, or classmates. It is a strange assumption we make when we think that Sally's friendship with Anna denies something to Maggie. What kids owe to one another is respect, not equal affections or equal treatment. Heretically, the same could be said of teachers and other institutional servants. Teachers should respect all their students, but beyond this they should be allowed their favorites.

Indeed, many parents are able to love all their children and also have favorites. The children may instinctively know who the favorite is, but if all the kids feel secure and loved, there is no significant resentment. We all know abuse cases, of course, where one child is spoiled and siblings are neglected. But that is just bad parenting, not a necessary consequence of favoritism.

Two kinds of equality are pursued under the title of egalitarianism. They are very different forms, but frequently mixed together—sometimes inadvertently and sometimes knowingly. *Equality of opportunity* is one form of egalitarianism, and *equality of outcomes* is another. The latter, equality of outcomes or shares, is often massaged into policies under the aegis of the former. While I am not opposed to equality of opportunity, I am opposed to rules and policies that attempt to create an equality of outcomes (especially when they violate merit and certain kinds of favoritism).

The confusion can be seen in the two elementary-school cases I've already mentioned. Trying to establish the equal *opportunity* of all kids for athletic activity, schools have mistakenly created an equal *outcomes* policy, in which all kids are given ribbons for "winning" the race. And trying to ensure an equal opportunity for kids to receive a gift or appreciation has twisted into an equal outcomes policy of mandatory valentines. In and of itself, these confusions are relatively harmless and the stakes are low. But as children are first inculcated with ideas and practices of fairness, these confusions stand as harbingers of things to come.

Instead of trying to square a circle, by transforming favoritism and meritocracy into fairness, we might try a more honest synthesis. A better way to integrate fairness and favoritism for kids is to show how *opportunity* and *outcome* are part of a process. Everyone should have equal *opportunity* to become your friend, but not everyone *can* be your friend (not everyone can *end up* as your friend). Anyone should be a candidate for friend status, but few will be admitted to the elite club. Why few? Because favorites (friends) can only be created by spending time together, sharing experiences, and immersing in each other's lives—and *time*, sadly, is a finite resource.

Treating opportunity and outcome as a *process* also thwarts the unfounded equation of preference and prejudice. Just because you prefer your favorites does not make you prejudiced. In the case of friendships, for example, kids should be encouraged to fish their friendships from the widest and most diverse pond available (using color-blind, gender-blind, and class-blind criteria), but then the resulting favorites will be a much smaller pool. Being discriminatory in your friendships is only prejudiced if you've *prejudged* candidates (pre-*judicare*). Judging *after* experience (post-judice) is justified preference, not prejudice.

I forget who made the funny and insightful quip about *good* books: Since I don't have enough time to read all the *great* books, I have no time for the merely good books. But something like this brutal truth applies to people too. Since I don't have enough time and affection for my crew of favorite people, I don't really have any time for strangers. I owe strangers courtesy, of course, but not much more.

5

The Circle of Favors
Global Perspectives

In 2005 I published a book about my adventures living in Cambodia. In this book I tried to show the spiritual altitudes of Khmer culture, the crushing poverty brought on by decades of political chaos, and the impressive character of the people. But it was not an overly sanguine, romanticized chronicle of Southeast Asia—in fact, I was careful to detail the dangerous side of a very corrupt country, where thugs flourish with impunity. Weapons are ubiquitous, as are drugs and prostitution, and I myself witnessed a brutal political assassination.

I was surprised, then, to receive an e-mail from a couple living in the United States, who claimed to be so inspired by my book that they were selling everything they owned and moving their whole family to Cambodia to help the poor. "Are you sure you read my book, and not some other?" I asked. But they were determined. They had nursing experience and wanted to offer their services to those suffering on the other side of the planet. I was further astounded to learn that they would be bringing along their young daughters to what I saw as dangers and privations. I shook my head in disbelief, but I held my breath and hoped for the best.

They sold their home and possessions and took their big hearts—and their innocent kids—into a jungle village in Cambodia, where they spent all their money on medical supplies and began attending to the staggering numbers of needy strangers. It is to their eternal credit that they helped many people in the few months after setting up shop. In short order, however, they began to make noise about local corruption and the almost nightly stealing of their medical supplies, and they naively sought redress through local political channels. Their humanitarian innocence did not go unpunished. The wife was run off the road one night by a group of politico thugs, who gang-raped and beat her—leaving her for dead. Sadly, this is a common method used by corrupt officials and local racketeers to "send a message" to reformers. Somehow the family managed to get to the capital city, where they frantically e-mailed me and others, explaining their dire situation: no money, an injured and suicidal mother, traumatized kids, and so on. My colleagues and I managed to get them connected to an excellent nongovernmental organization (NGO) that probably saved their lives and got them back to the States. Happily, they all survived this heartbreaking ordeal.

When a culture like ours combines the secular grid of impartiality with the saintly ideals of Good Samaritan selflessness, a unique form of philanthropy emerges. Charity takes this odd form in the developed West—and we're so accustomed to it in the United States that we confuse our idiosyncratic humanitarian impulse with the good itself. I will refer to the uniquely Western philanthropists as the "world-savers," because their goodwill extends so far beyond the usual tribal circles. This American couple who dragged their kids to Cambodia to heal the strangers were "world-savers." They may be guilty of something philosopher Christina Hoff Sommers calls the "Jellyby fallacy"—named after Mrs. Jellyby in Dickens's *Bleak House*, a "telescopic philanthropist" who cares more for a faraway African tribe than her own family.[1] One is struck by the parallels with certain Hollywood celebrities who have adopted a veritable United Nations of children from around the world, championed every noble humanitarian cause, but somehow can't find compassion enough to reconcile with their own estranged parents or siblings. These strange fallacies of misplaced loyalty are not attempts at fairness per se, but aberrant mutations born of the fairness impulse (seeking to de-privilege kin and redistribute benefits to strangers).

Is it any wonder that Westerners are susceptible to the Jellyby fallacy, when Christianity tells us: "God so loved the world that he sacrificed his only son for us"? It may be pious and mystically beautiful to sacrifice your son for others, but it's also transcendently bad parenting.

The "world-savers" are very familiar to us in the States, and they contrast strongly with the "favoritists." The East and the West share common notions of saintly altruism, but the East never adopted the grid of impartiality. Consequently, the East is more clannish, more favoritist, in their ethical convictions. In the fall of 2010, for example, Bill Gates and Warren Buffet made a trip to Beijing to promote the idea of philanthropy. China's rocketing economy has created around 900,000 new millionaires (U.S. dollar equivalent) in recent years, but Chinese culture has never really promoted or understood the idea of spreading wealth to strangers. To an uneducated American, this looks retrograde and callous, but it really just reveals the value-system difference that I've been exploring. Chinese culture puts things like loyalty and filial piety far above values like fairness and egalitarianism. American billionaires Gates and Buffet were met with some trepidation and skepticism in Beijing, because Chinese notions of charity strongly privilege family over strangers—they are favoritists, not world-savers.

Chinese Favoritism

The "East" is of course a diverse region, made up of many different cultures, ethnicities, and political frameworks. But two very deep root systems tunnel under all that diversity: (1) Confucianism in the Far East (in China, Korea, Japan, and Vietnam), and (2) Indian cosmology, especially caste systems (in India, Pakistan, Sri Lanka, Burma, Laos, Thailand, and Cambodia). Obviously Arab culture has its own deep filial tribalism—for example, one recalls the Arab adage "My brother and me against my cousin; me, my brother, and my cousin against the stranger." But for my purposes here, I want to focus on Chinese and then Indian culture because they so clearly contrast with our own culture of fairness.

Kongzi, or Confucius, gave us our nice example—back in chapter 1—of the son who virtuously shelters the thieving father. We should look now at the filial piety system that produces this brand of favoritism virtue. Filial piety, or *xiao*, is deep respect for parents and ancestors, and when Chinese people talk of *xiao*, they're usually referring to the obligations, duties, and sacrifices that children (especially the elder son) must fulfill toward aging parents. But the concept of filial piety is also bigger and includes the many duties that family members have toward one another—parents, children, siblings, uncles, nephews, nieces, grandparents. A person who puts himself above the interests of his family is not dutiful, and a person who puts non-relations above the interests of his family is quite possibly insane.

It is hard for Westerners to appreciate *xiao*, or parent duty, in the same way as the Chinese, because for us parents are just "one case" or "example" of the people who fall under our general rules of ethical duty. We think of ethics as grid-like: a good person does not lie, he doesn't lie to his neighbor, and he doesn't lie to his parents. It is "lying" or "truth telling" that must be applied to various social interactions. The *rule* dominates, and *persons* are just variables under the rule. For Chinese people, it is different. Ethical duties don't *apply* to parents; ethical duties themselves *come from* parent-child bonds. The book of filial piety *Xiao Jing* (c. 400 BCE) is attributed to Kongzi, and when Confucianism was adopted as the state philosophy (during the Han Dynasty), the book was required reading for all imperial and civil officials (until 1911). Chapter 1 of *Xiao Jing* states, "*Xiao* is the foundation of virtue, and is what all teaching grows out of."[2] Unlike many other cultures, Chinese ethics is not divine or supernatural. It is based on the secular idealism of family relationships.

"He who loves his parents," *Xiao Jing* explains, "does not dare to do evil unto others; he who respects his parents does not dare to be arrogant to others. Love and respect are exerted to the utmost in serving

Fig. 15. Kongzi (Confucius) (551–479 bc) contoured the East Asian mind with positive favoritism and built ethics on a secular platform of benevolent bias. Drawing by Stephen Asma.

the parents, and this virtue and teaching is extended to the people."[3] Loyalty and respect flow upward, downward, and around again. A father shows respect and affection to his wife and children, who in turn serve the father (with work, affection, and resources) that he then uses to better serve his parents. A micro circle of beneficence is created in the nuclear family that radiates out toward the social macrocosm. And rulers, or those in power, are also expected to live by this circle of respect, loyalty, and affection.[4] *Xiao* inside the family is the incubator for love, respect, and loyalty outside the family. *Xiao* teaches us how to serve others.

The high importance of family in Chinese sociopolitical culture can be seen in the etymology of their word for "nation": *guojia*—a combination of *guo* (state) and *jia* (family). The tribalism of family loyalty provides an informal social security system, including help for unemployed, sick, or disabled kin and resources for education—and blood-related children will often be transferred to the most prosperous uncle's family to be raised (Chinese frequently "adopt" kin in this way, but rarely adopt strangers in the way that Westerners do).

The obligation to parents is so foundational that it is even required by Chinese law. The Chinese constitution requires children to care for their elderly parents. "It is inconceivable and incomprehensible to the Chinese to see how people in the West, particularly those well-to-do, put their aged parents in nursing homes. To them, it is simply an unforgivable sin."[5]

Shortly after I returned from China, I was on an author's panel at a book fair in Chicago. One of the panelists had written a book on the challenges of caring for elderly parents in contemporary America, and she assured the anxious audience that "taking care of your elderly parents is a *choice*, not an obligation. *You don't have to do it.*" I could not then, nor can I now, imagine a more antithetical sentiment to Chinese ethics.

Today *xiao* continues to define the Asian worldview well beyond the borders of China. Preferential treatment, or biased partiality, is not just "tolerated" in Asian ethics—it is required. Favoritism is the groundwork of Confucian culture. The model of the good person is not the saintly world-saver, but the devoted family member. As for the Jellyby fallacy, *Xiao Jing* clearly states, "He who does not love his parents but loves others, we call that perverse virtue. For he who does not respect his parents but respects others, we call that perverse courtesy."[6]

The practice of filial piety extends out beyond the family and becomes a related form of social lubricant called *guanxi*. I introduced this idea in chapter 1, but here we see it in a fuller context. Often translated as "social connection" or "close relationship," if I have good *guanxi*, then I have strong and influential social connections. I can get things done, because I know the right people and they look out for me. It is crucial to build up good *guanxi* in life, because you will always need a circle of favorites.

This system of *guanxi* favoritism runs counter to the bureaucracies of modernity. The modern Western grid of fairness is partly produced by and protected by bureaucracy—impartial rules and regulations that ignore persons. *Guanxi*, by contrast, is explicitly personal. The system of favoritism works if you live in a "face culture."

Face Culture

I have spent a lot of time traveling in China and even lived in the Chinese district of Shanghai in 2007.[7] There were very few *waiguoren* (or foreigners) in my neighborhood—I sometimes heard myself referred to as a *gweilo*—which means "white ghost" and is an informal but rather inoffensive way of calling me a foreigner.

Downtown Shanghai is crawling with *gweilo*, and my presence never registered a second look when I walked down the city streets, but out in the hinterland of my neighborhood, I could attract a small crowd of slack-jawed spectators. And if I was walking with my three-year old son (half-*gweilo*, half-Chinese), people would regularly stop, point, crane their necks, and even get in bicycle accidents in order to examine his little exotic face. Happily, all this hyper-attention was positive. In my experience, the Chinese are not xenophobic, but very xeno-curious.

My son, whose mother is Chinese, was a constant source of excitement. And Chinese folks on the street (especially older folks) would analyze his face in detail—usually pointing out his large eyes and other such physiognomic nuances. It freaked him out a little to have people so intensely interested in him (even touching his face and breaching every Western norm of personal space), but eventually he got used to it.

But how your *face* appears to others is not just an aesthetic issue in China; it is a deep social and cultural metaphor. Saving face, losing face, giving face: these are all important aspects of Chinese social graces, and I learned much more about it living in the hinterlands than in the commercialized (and frankly Westernized) downtown.

In face culture, you must "be somebody" in order to get privileges— you must have merit appeal (achieved excellence) or you must know the right people (*guanxi*). And while this nepotism horrifies most Americans because it seems exclusionary, I hasten to add that both boarding passes—accomplishment and *guanxi*—are considered to be entirely within your reach (Confucianism believes that effort and discipline solve most social disadvantages).

Giving face, or causing someone to lose face, can be very subtle. And for an unrefined Chicago boy like myself, it was like tiptoeing through a minefield of possible infractions. A certain tone of voice should be used with elders; gifts should be brought when arriving at certain events, sometimes specific foods, sometimes (like at a wedding) very specific amounts of money; a myriad of different titles must be used to address everyone from taxi drivers to professors to one's aunts and uncles; particular kinds of compliments must be used for certain people. In many cases, one doesn't "compliment" directly but rather learns the art of "precision insults" in order to give face to one's friend. For example, if your friend is struggling feebly with some electronic device or maybe some stubborn merchandise packaging, you should hurl insults at the difficult item and its idiotic manufacturers. You should not, in most cases, just step in to do it yourself, because if you manage the problem easily, then you have caused your friend to lose face.

As a *gweilo*, I marched and stumbled unwittingly, like a bull in a china shop, through all these delicate face matters (*mianzi*). But I was usually given a pass because, as an American, I was expected to be uncultured. Once, a Chinese friend came to our house with a gift for my son, and I made the mistake of offering her a seat at the dinner table. To my mind this was a kindly act of goodwill, but because we were already halfway into our meal, my gesture was perceived as an insulting offer to eat our leftovers.

Unlike in Chicago, or America generally, the Chinese don't think everyone is equal. America may not *really* be an egalitarian country, but it certainly likes to pretend it is. Egalitarian fairness, however, is not even an ideal in China—never has been. As a teacher, for example, I was treated with ridiculous amounts of respect. In Confucian cultures like China (and Cambodia, where I also lived and taught), I was treated with far more respect than I ever experienced in the States (where you're treated more like the French-fry cook at a fast-food drive-thru). It is the legacy of our Socratic education system that leads Westerners to always challenge authority and treat it with suspicion; but in a Confucian culture, authority figures, people of rank, and elderly people are assumed to be sources of wisdom (until proven otherwise). Our cultures have two different starting points when thinking about social hierarchy.[8]

One of the things that I didn't understand about Chinese culture before I lived there was that this stress on saving face and having status in other's eyes are wedded to a strong emphasis on communal ethics. The public culture of status applies to everything, not just your job, education, or economic status, but even your moral status. And your goal is to work hard to improve that status. From Confucius to Mao, there is an emphasis on *public ethics* rather than the private, inner guilt-based ethics of the West. A Westerner—who is accustomed to the private, intimate sense of values—will be very surprised to find perfect strangers in China suggesting moral improvements to you in public.

Walking through the streets of our neighborhood, we were regularly scolded by perfect strangers. Scowling women, working in markets or passing by, would examine our son carefully, look up at his mother (again as a *gweilo* I usually got a pass), and tell her, without irony or humor, that she was a bad mother because our son was too skinny. He needed to be fattened up! Then we would be regaled with a litany of fat-producing recipes, usually involving an elaborate turtle soup or a special chicken-fat concoction. The reprimand from these strangers was surprising at first, and no attempt was made to hide their moral judgment. On the contrary, they felt (and this is common in a face culture) that they were improving us, and more importantly improving our son. My wife, born and raised on the Mainland, was never surprised or offended by these public harassments.

Imagine strolling up to a family on the street in Chicago and lecturing the parents about the sad state of their obese kids. I can actually hear your face getting slapped. In our culture, we're taught to disregard what others think of us because our personal value is supposed to be independent of social recognition. The Chinese, however, do not share the assumption (codified in Christianity and secular human rights) that every individual is autonomous and intrinsically valuable. An individual's value is socially defined, so the creation of a *favoritism circle* is crucial both for one's career and, more fundamentally, one's very identity.[9]

In addition to an emphasis on public ethics, Chinese people also think more in terms of moral heroes. Instead of our Western view of ethics as the impartial application of universal rules, the Chinese think about paragon characters—persons, not principles. The *junzi*, for example, is the Confucian "superior person"—noble, modest, caring, wise, and magnanimous.

The *junzi* can be contrasted with the *xiaoren*, which means "small person" or petty. The better you are in your tribal duties to family, the better you are at building good *guanxi* outside the family, and then the better you are as a citizen and even as a politician. These forms of favoritism actually make you a *junzi*, superior person, and this good character feeds back into your generous daily dealings with others. The powerful person is required to be the benevolent person. A well-known Chinese idiom describes the magnanimous *junzi* as "so big that he can float a boat inside his belly" (*zai xiang du li neng cheng chuan*). The Western conflation of nepotism and corruption is premised on the assumption that power corrupts, but Confucianism suggests that proper education prevents such abuses.

Confucian culture, then, holds out an impressive alternative to our fairness culture. Those who think that the grid of impartiality is either inevitable, preordained, or unparalleled have billions of people and thousands of years to explain away. The idea that modern ethics must be centered on fairness reminds me of Evangelicals who claim that all ethics must be centered on monotheism. All of Chinese culture, with its secular favoritism, stands as a staggering contradiction to both narrow claims.

Indian Favoritism

In a recent study of global ethics, 76 percent of Indian college students thought that "insider trading" on the stock market was "completely fair" or "acceptable."[10] Only 36 percent of U.S. students considered the same case to be ethically acceptable (in the United States, such trading is only illegal if the trade was done *before* relevant information becomes public). This does not indicate an Indian lack of ethics, but rather a different framework of ethics. The finance professor who analyzed this data, aptly named Statman, adopted the same old false dichotomy, when he asked, "Why are people different from one another in their tilt toward self-interest or fairness, and why are people of one country different, on average, from people of another?" Of course, the question of why some countries are more fair-minded is a good one, but—as I've been arguing—"self-interest" is not the proper contrasting opposite. Tribal devotion, filial piety, and kin bias are much more accurate contraries to fairness. I would suggest that the high percentage of Indian acceptance of insider trading reflects tribal family values—which are very strong in India—rather than individualistic self-interest. Kin-based cultures, like India, do not place much trust in people/institutions outside the family, and they privilege insider information and interests. In fact, if the true contrast was between individual selfishness and fairness, as Meir Statman assumes, then we might expect to see a reverse of the percentage figures. After all, American Nobel Prize–winning economist Milton Friedman—a free-market individualist—argued explicitly for *more* insider trading, not *less*.

I submit that Indian people are comfortable with the insider trading case and a variety of other cases that Westerners would call "conflicts of interest" because India (like China) never adopted the grid of impartiality. India, despite being the world's biggest democracy, is not an egalitarian culture.

Nobel laureate and India-born scholar Amartya Sen thinks we shouldn't make too much of the cultural differences between East and West.[11] The Buddha, he reminds us, was thoroughly Indian, but also thoroughly devoted to egalitarian opportunities for enlightenment.[12] This much is true, but Sen forgets to mention that the Buddha—being extremely heterodox in both metaphysics and social theory—did not contour the Indian mind in any significant way.[13] Contrary to Sen, I would say that egalitarianism has "flickered" in Indian culture, but it has not dominated. Sen is at pains to bring Indian culture into the Western conversation and legitimize it by celebrating these "flickers," whereas I am actually a fan of nepotistic favoritism and see no need to apologize for it.

Fig. 16. The Laws of Manu, composed between 200 BCE and 200 CE, codify traditional Indian thinking on moral, social, and legal matters. The laws (which are highly exceptional rather than universal) are considered to be a direct transmission from the supreme progenitor of humankind, Manu. In this depiction, Vishnu (in fish form) warns Manu to prepare for a coming flood that will wipe out everything. Drawing by Stephen Asma, based on traditional Indian representations.

A more accurate assessment of the relevant cultural difference is A. K. Ramanujan's claim that Hindu dharma (law) is *context dependent* and slightly different from caste to caste.[14] Traditional Indian culture has not recognized a one-size-fits-all universal moral code—like we see in Kant's categorical imperative or utilitarian metrics. There is no grid of impartiality in Indian culture. The Laws of Manu (*Manava Dharmasastra*), composed between 200 BCE and 200 CE, codify traditional Indian thinking on moral, social, and legal matters. Manu's laws are considered to be a direct transmission from the supreme progenitor of humankind. Manu says that a king "who knows the sacred law, must imagine [his way] into the laws of caste, of districts, of guilds, and of families, and thus settle the peculiar laws of each" (Manu 7:41). As Ramanujan describes it, "To be moral, for Manu, is to particularize— to ask who did what, to whom and when."[15]

Traditional Indian culture accepts the idea that social life is filled with inconsistencies and exceptions. The caste hierarchy, for example, goes from Brahmans on top, to Kshatriyas below, to Vaishyas below that, to Sudras below that. The Laws of Manu tell us, for example, that a Kshatriya who defames a Brahmin will be fined one hundred coins, but a Vaishya who defames a Brahmin will be fined two hundred coins. And exceptionalism applies to virtues too. Ramanujan quotes German philosopher Hegel, who noted: "While we say 'Bravery is a virtue,' the Hindus say, on the contrary, 'Bravery is a virtue of the Kshatriyas [the warrior caste].'" Moreover, it is common in Indian culture to think of morally good conduct as age-specific. The moral life of the middle-aged householder is quite different from the morally righteous path of the elderly person, and so on. For example, a middle-aged parent is duty bound to expend most of their energy providing for their children, not chasing after enlightenment. But when the same parent's children are full-grown, he is now morally expected to turn toward the ascetic purification of his own soul. It is also common to accept the relativity of, or contextual relevance of, geographic region. It is accepted that in the North, the southern ways would be wrong and vice versa.[16]

My point here is not to celebrate the caste system. Supernatural cosmic maps of "favorite" classes are absurd and untenable in the modern world. They are absurd for several reasons. One, the speculative metaphysics of Vedantic religious scriptures should not dictate contemporary social structure, because those scriptures (like our zodiac or perhaps our own Western scriptures) are pre-scientific, outmoded attempts to understand nature. We have much better methods for understanding nature now. Two, the caste categories are rigid and non-negotiable (pursuant to their supernatural status), whereas more permeable social boundaries (merit-based or otherwise) are much more consistent with human flourishing.

What I am suggesting, instead, is that Indian culture embraces the contextual differences of value that are intrinsic to human interaction. This entails the more healthy forms of favoritism like kin nepotism, family bias, tribal loyalty, preference of friends over colleagues over strangers, and so on. They don't attempt to mash down these unfair topographies with a universal grid of impartiality. They accept them as part of the good life. The imbalances are inside the moral life, not outside it.

The most immediate context for the context-sensitive Indian is family. The psychologist Alan Roland has suggested that Indians carry their family context wherever they go.[17] Indians, Chinese, and other Asians possess a stronger "familial self"—a constant sense of continuity with family. The individual already contains a little circle of benefactors, cohorts, dependents—favorites, by birth or choice, who will always receive biased attention and consideration.

A touching example of this filial favoritism—so strong in Asian cultures—can be detected in the notes scrawled by tsunami survivor Hiromitsu Shinkawa. He was found ten miles out to sea, floating on the roof of his house, after the devastating 2011 Tohoku earthquake in Japan. After floating for two days without rescue, Shinkawa—believing that he would soon be dead—began scrawling notes for posterity (using a marker he found floating in the water). He scribbled a few notes to his elderly parents, regretting his own untimely demise and the fact that he would not be able to take care of them in the future: "I am sorry for being unfilial." Sometime later, floating on the slowly sinking debris, he wrote: "I'm in a lot of trouble. Sorry for dying before you. Please forgive me."[18]

In sum, then, the filial piety cultures of Asia hold out an impressive alternative to our fairness culture of disinterested equality. They celebrate favoritism and see ethics as an extension of it, rather than an opponent to morality. If ethics and justice are equated with fairness, then half the world is reprobate. Obviously I think the problem is in our impoverished Western notion of the good, not in Asian cultures.[19]

Disentangling Nepotism and Corruption

Many of us assume that biased nepotistic behavior is intrinsically corrupt and needs to be rooted out wherever it grows. We see the democratization of power, decision making, and wealth as good insurance against greed and abuse. Americans, influenced by Montesquieu's political philosophy, tend to think of power in terms of checks and balances. Two main counterweights seem necessary to us for balancing corrupt power. One is the decentralization of power. Make sure the persons in charge cannot act in a purely executive manner—hence the three branches of government. We seek to spread power through multiple individuals or groups. And, two, make sure that the powerful persons have no *interest* in the cases they oversee—hence judges recuse themselves from cases considered too close to them. Disinterest (that great Enlightenment term) is crucial as a guarantee that the leader will not funnel profits into his particular coffers.

These assumptions are so deep in the Western mind that doubting them seems heretical. The quest for disinterested power, for example, is so old that even Plato—who hated democracy and egalitarianism—nonetheless argued that the only reason why his philosopher kings could be trusted with the utopian republic was because they didn't *want* to rule. Plato's philosopher kings only govern begrudgingly—they are utterly disinterested in mundane profit, wealth, and honor, and would rather be meditating on the pure Forms of knowledge.

Hopefully, my short tour of Eastern values has primed us to question our usual assumptions about decentralized and disinterested power. A whole other way of thinking about power has been suppressed and covered over by the grid of impartiality. If we change from thinking of ethics as rules, or even individual actions, we begin to appreciate *agent centered* ethics. In this agent-centered tradition, the good is not some calculus or distribution of deserts, but the actions of a virtuous character. In China, we see it in the Confucian tradition of the magnanimous *junzi*—powerful but benevolent. In Southeast Asia, we find the *dhammaraja*, the virtuous monarch. In the ancient West, we find it in Aristotle's view of the "great-souled man."

The idea that one can be both powerful *and* benevolent is highly suspicious to many egalitarians. But every nuclear family is an obvious example of concentrated parental power and flourishing benefactor children. A father's care for his children is the real counterweight to his power—and if he has good character, his power goes entirely toward the well-being of his dependents. The benevolent use of power inside the nuclear family is just an illustration of the fact that unfair power distribution does not automatically entail unjust and unhappy conditions. Are there bad fathers who abuse their power? Sadly, yes. Does this mean that fatherhood is intrinsically corrupt, and patriarchs should step aside?

The revolutionary communist and writer for the *Revolution* newspaper, Sunsara Taylor, recently scolded me during a public radio debate. The nuclear family, she told me, was the incubator for all abuse, corruption, and exploitation—the institutionalized headquarters of rape and oppression. Ms. Taylor's draconian view represents the Revolutionary Communist Party, USA, which still takes a Maoist line on the evils of the nuclear family. For them, the favoritism inherent in family life must be broken, so that affection, devotion, and wealth can be evenly distributed throughout the party.[20]

I'll avoid the ad hominem temptation to muse on Ms. Taylor's own childhood and instead focus on the philosophical error, as I see it. Many people have pointed out that abolishing the family, in the service of fairness, runs counter to human nature and is therefore doomed to failure. It should be obvious, given chapter 2, that I agree with the spirit of this critique. Nonetheless, I want to highlight a different conceptual issue, not just the pragmatic failure of anti-filial policy.

Abolishing the nuclear family, and fathers in particular, is also premised on the assumption that power corrupts (and should be decentralized). Both communists (regarding the family) and liberals (regarding the politician) assume that selfish exploitation is the default position for human beings. But the agent-centered ethics of Aristotle and Confucius see selfishness as the exceptional or pathological case, not the norm. Aristotle argues that the selfish man is like a spoiled child.[21] Most fathers and mothers are benevolent power centers, not spoiled selfish exploiters. We should not use the exceptions (bad parents) to abolish the rule (parenthood). Since parents are probably the first and most devoted nepotists of all, it seems relevant to my argument to celebrate them as neither corrupt nor intrinsically exploitative. We should not use the *abuses* of nepotism to damn nepotism per se.[22] Even at the governmental level, some autocrats use their concentrated power well and some badly.[23] The jury is still out, but it's relatively safe to say that

Zimbabwe's Robert Mugabe has practiced nepotism in unjust ways, but Rwanda's Paul Kagame has a better track record. And historically speaking, Cyrus the Great (585–529 BC) had a relatively decent track record, as did Constantine the Great (c. 272–337 CE).[24]

Now, the other major reason why Westerners see nepotistic favoritism as corrupt is because they cannot envisage a scenario where the *interests* or benefits of a superior can coexist with the interests of her subordinates. A good ruler is supposed to be personally disinterested, otherwise she cannot help her subjects properly. This view has colored political theory from Plato's philosopher kings, through Enlightenment egalitarianism, and down to John Rawls's theory of fairness. The truly fair person, according to this tradition of disinterest, is the one who acts with a blind eye (or a "veil of ignorance") toward her own advantage. A ruler, manager, or any policy-making moral agent must not be distracted by the wants and needs of her own family, because such distraction will compromise benefits for the wider population.

My own view is that this is sanctimonious twaddle. Not every beneficent action is a zero-sum game; in fact, many different kinds of gains are compatible with one another. We assume that all such cases are "conflicts of interest," but frequently they are not. One person's gain is not automatically a loss for another person. It is entirely possible for a ruler to benefit *both* his daughter and the wider population by appointing a capable daughter to a position of power. If you're on the Left, for example, you might recognize that Senator Al Gore Sr. helped both his son, Al Gore, and the country by furthering Al's political career. If you're on the Right, you might say the same about George H. Bush and George W. Bush. My point is not to resolve which of these nepotistic events was better for the country, but to illustrate the *compatibility* between acting for the tribe and acting for the wider population.

A political philosopher who was perceptive enough, and honest enough, to drop the pretensions of disinterest was Machiavelli (1469–1527). The Italian philosopher is often misunderstood and demonized precisely because we assume, yet again, the false dichotomy between ethics and self-interest. Since Machiavelli frequently encourages the ruler to engage in manipulations (e.g., the ruler must be a fox as well as a lion), he is usually misinterpreted to be a self-centered, self-serving tyrant. In fact, even a cursory reading of *The Prince* reveals a ruler who is utterly devoted to his own people and willing to get into the gutter in order to serve them best. Yes, there are many power machinations recommended in *The Prince*, but they are for the benefit of the people as much as the prince and kin (e.g., the purpose of plundering foreign territories, he argues, is to create wealth and relieve tax burdens for your own people—not just for the coffers of the rulers). In realpolitik, personal and public advantage are not mutually exclusive.

But enough about princes, kings, and subjects. What about the nepotism down at my office, at my company, or in my trade or profession? Recent reports suggest that almost 90 percent of American businesses are family owned. Nepotism has also risen dramatically as women have filled the workplace—increasing the probability of romantic relationships, marriage, and partner favoritism at work. Researcher Bridgette Kaye Harder says that nepotism is extensive, but it is "one of the least studied and most poorly understood human resource practices in business today."[25]

Anxiety about favoritism and the imminent threat of discrimination litigation led American businesses to enact "anti-nepotism policies" in the 1950s. But many of these anti-nepotism policies, aimed at greater equity, actually created new discrimination. When it was discovered that a married couple was working together, the more junior of the two was usually terminated (citing reasons of experience and seniority). This meant that married female employees were disproportionately harmed by anti-nepotism policies, and counter-litigation exploded in the 1980s. Companies generally responded to all this expensive litigation by relaxing their nepotism policies in the 1990s, and our contemporary business climate continues this laissez-faire approach.

In 2003 a series of research studies, together with Adam Bellow's *In Praise of Nepotism*, argued that nepotism had real advantages in the business world.[26] More kin at work increases the transfer of knowledge and contacts, increases communication generally, and also increases employee satisfaction and commitment. In summary, then, there is good reason—both logical and empirical—for rejecting the assumption that favoritism is tantamount to corruption.

Disentangling Tribalism and Tragedy

In the West, one often finds a facile equation of tribalism and violence. Some versions of liberalism seek to eliminate all tribal tendencies, arguing that tribalism separates rather than unifies us. Violence in the Middle East and Africa, for example, is often chalked up to an inevitable consequence of tribal societies. Adding to this general viewpoint is the common assumption that tribalism is an evolutionary fossil—a form of social organization that helped us on the Pleistocene plains of Africa but lingers now like a vestigial organ. Tribalism, it is often assumed, is the outmoded "appendix" or "wisdom tooth" of the social organism. I agree with the claims of when and why tribalism first evolved, but I do not share the condescension about its contemporary value.

General skepticism about tribalism has become almost dogmatic. It oversimplifies the real causes of violence and social unrest, shedding little light on unique sociohistorical complexities. It also pretends at moral superiority, all the while denying our own tribal affiliations.

Still, there is indeed a bloody catalog of horror stories that seem instigated, or at least fueled, by tribal differences. Mongols, Native Americans, Aztecs, Catholics, Protestants, Crusaders, Amazonian Yanomami, and New Zealand Maori—just to name a few—all seemed fueled by what Freud called the "narcissism of minor differences." One of the most horrific tribal slaughters in recent memory occurred in Rwanda, between the Tutsi and the Hutu. But was tribalism per se to blame, or was tribalism simply one of the avenues of aggression and exploitation?

I spent time in Rwanda in 2010 and was astounded (as I had been in Cambodia) by the resilience, dignity, and genuine warmth of the people. It is humbling when you get to know people who have suffered so dramatically. It inspires you to overcome your own relatively minor problems and to appreciate the heroism and grace that emerges

Fig. 17. The 1994 Rwandan genocide involved Hutu and Tutsi and led to the mass killing of approximately 800,000 people in one hundred days. Skulls are tragically displayed at the Kigali Memorial Centre. Drawing by Stephen Asma.

spontaneously under such pressure. But make no mistake, Rwanda is still a land of nightmares—terrible dreams and memories, haunting almost everyone you encounter. A visit to the Kigali Memorial Centre will give you a few souvenir nightmares of your own.

I became friends with a Rwandan man named John, who had lost most of his family during the genocide. He had gone to study in Uganda in the early 1990s and became trapped there during the complex civil war. Eventually, he was forced to fight in the Ugandan army and saw many horrors of his own. When he returned home after the genocide, he found his parents and siblings had been killed. His old rival neighbors were living in his childhood home. With the help of his military connections, he retook his own property and slowly rebuilt a life for himself—eventually marrying and starting a family.

When I asked him, one day, if he was Tutsi or Hutu, he laughed and said, "I cannot tell you that, my friend. It is against the law to reveal my ethnicity to you." Eventually, I could discern his tribe from other things he told me about his history, but the lesson is that one's tribal affiliation is not written on the body by obvious physical traits. Why is it now forbidden to broadcast one's tribe in Rwanda?

Between April and July 1994, an estimated 800,000 Rwandans brutally murdered each other, often cutting each other down with machetes. The UN failed to give its own commander the manpower and approval to mitigate the disaster, and the wider world stood by while the slaughter took place. Majority Hutu were attacking minority Tutsi—trying to wipe them off the earth. The violence targeted Tutsi, but Hutu killed many other Hutu as well. American pundits chalked up the disaster to inevitable tribal warfare.

There were indeed old tensions between the tribes. Minority Tutsi had ruled over majority Hutu for centuries before German and then Belgian colonialism. During the colonial period (1890s–1950s), Tutsi remained in power, both facilitating and benefiting from colonial interests. As independence unfolded, in the late 1950s and early 1960s, Hutu power grew and eventually replaced the traditional Tutsi monarchy with a Hutu republic—which straightaway began persecuting Tutsi.

In the 1970s Hutu general Juvénal Habyarimana seized power and increased the campaign of abuse and degradation toward the Tutsi, fearmongering the majority into paranoia about Tutsi plans to enslave Hutu. None of this typical strongman political manipulation would have been possible if the Belgians had not previously dramatized and exacerbated tribal differences—forcing everyone to carry separate tribal ID cards.

Divide-and-conquer techniques proved so effective during colonial rule, that Habyarimana and his allies continued the practice, introducing mass-media publications and radio broadcasts that demonized Tutsi as "cockroaches."[27] In the early 1990s, the government began stockpiling weapons and training killing militias to wipe out the "scheming" Tutsi "threat" walking among them. Neighbors eyed neighbors suspiciously, and Hutu listened to unfounded radio conspiracy theories about Tutsi torturing and killing the Hutu president of Burundi. Then, when distrust was at a fever pitch, Habyarimana's plane was mysteriously shot down in April 1994, and violence exploded around the country—setting off a hundred days of horrifying genocidal bloodshed. When I asked my friend John how neighbors could so viciously kill neighbors, often raping and torturing them, he said, "The people were brainwashed. The people could not see the humanity in their enemies—they saw them as monsters or demons."[28]

Tribal tension is not the only explanation for the genocide. When I stayed at the Sabyinyo Silverback Lodge, I had dinner with the manager Bernard De Wetter, whose life in the Rwanda jungles coils all the way back to his days as a researcher in Dian Fossey's Karisoke Research Center. "The underlying problem in Rwanda is overpopulation," Bernard explained. "I doubt that you'll ever a see a genocide in Botswana, for example, where there is plenty of space. You hate your neighbor? Fine, no problem—just move. There's plenty of land and resources in Botswana. But not in Rwanda." Bernard added ominously, "This may become a problem again soon, because 70 percent of Rwanda is under twenty-five years old and trying to make their way in a low-resource situation."

Anthropologist Jared Diamond's Malthusian interpretation of the Rwandan genocide takes its start from the fact that population growth increased more rapidly than food production in the post-colonial era.[29] From the 1960s to the late 1980s, populations spiked, as did short-term agricultural practices that ultimately eroded topsoil and compromised irrigation. This led to famines in the late 1980s and early 1990s. Larger farms had off-farm incomes that allowed them to buy up smaller farms, thereby radically increasing the divide between the haves and the have-nots. All this led to a social context of hunger, suspicion, and desperation—perfect chaos into which old ethnic differences could be introduced as simplistic subterfuges for more complex economic ecological problems. When the genocide broke out in 1994, many killings failed to fit into the ethnic interpretation of the conflict but did conform to the economic interpretation. Professor Diamond quotes sociologists C. Andre and J. Platteau as saying, "The 1994 events provided a unique opportunity to settle scores, or to reshuffle land properties, even among Hutu villagers. . . . It is not rare, even today, to hear Rwandans argue that a war is necessary to wipe out an excess of population and bring numbers into line with the available resources."[30]

My goal in introducing this Malthusian interpretation is not to suggest some form of Darwinian determinism (i.e., populations that outstrip their resources must engage in warfare). The Rwandan genocide is a multi-caused phenomenon, with many intersecting variables. But I introduce this ecological interpretation to complicate and throw skepticism on the purely ethnic interpretation of the violence. Economics and ecology played a bigger role than tribalism in the conditions that led up to the genocide. Moreover, tribal hostility itself was exacerbated by colonial powers that sought to destabilize the region for easier exploitation of Rwandan resources.

In taking on this "worst-case scenario" of Rwandan genocide, I'm arguing two things. One, the tribal distinctions between the Hutu and Tutsi were not destined to result in genocidal violence. History shows that the ethnic tribalism was not overly pugilistic until colonial powers intensified hostilities and mass media invented hysteria. Why bother making this argument? Because my own view is that human distinctions of "us and them" are probably inevitable, but hostility is not. Trying to get rid of the latter by eliminating the former is a common liberal mistake. I share the desire to eliminate intergroup hostility, but I don't think it will come from a denial or rejection of our group biases. We should remember, after all, that egalitarianism (i.e., communism and democracy) did far more bloodletting in the twentieth century than tribalism.

Second, by disentangling tribalism and tragedy, I'm making room for a middle way—one that preserves favoritism and group bias, but diminishes intergroup violence and hostility. One of the main reasons why ethnic cleansing takes on such ferocity in cases like Rwanda, Bosnia, or even Hitler's Germany is because tribal differences (ethnic or cultural) become spiritualized or divinized. Metaphysics sneaks into the picture and renders minor differences into melodramatic schisms. You're not one of us, the ideology proclaims, and the entire cosmos has decreed it!

My view is that metaphysical tribalism is dangerous nonsense. There is a big difference between saying, "I was accidentally born into this quirky family, so they're my inner tribe" and "My Brahmin de-

scendants flowed from the sacrificed head of the cosmic being Pu-
rusha, so Brahmins are my tribe." The social behaviors, and forms of
favoritism, that flow from these two views are quite different. Racial
forms of tribalism are also dangerous, but thankfully not inevitable.[31]
    Group solidarity is highly malleable. Humans may come with some
preset or default in-group loyalties (i.e., the nuclear family), but they
can rebrand their own group identities with relative ease. This malleability, especially strong in cosmopolitan cultures, demonstrates the
artificial rigidity of metaphysical and racial forms of tribalism. So, part
of my middle-way position is to call for *better* tribes, not the inflexible,
metaphysical kind. Since I don't think tribes inevitably end in tragedy,
I need some criteria for distinguishing good ones from bad ones. One
such criterion is ready to hand: whenever tribes assign themselves *supernatural merit*, we're probably in for big trouble.

It's important to close this section by drawing together several strands
of international practices and attitudes to offer another case of "ethical
favoritism." Since most Western philosophers see "ethical favoritism"
as an oxymoron, I have been at pains throughout this book to point
out cases to the contrary, like family loyalty, beneficent nepotism, or
friendship. Now I want to briefly describe a common practice in developing continents like Asia and Africa. It is the practice of "sponsorship" or "patronage."
    When my Rwandan friend John and I traveled near his home vil-
lage, he stopped the car at the sight of a small elderly man who was
sitting by the side of the road. John leaped out of the car, and the two
greeted each other warmly and spoke for a while before John returned
and explained that this was his pygmy friend Habimana. John was
Habimana's sponsor, he explained. John had encountered him a few
years ago—he discovered the pygmy broke, hungry, and begging to
support himself and his daughter. Over time he and old Habimana
became friends, and John—a man of very little means himself—took
on the role of sponsor.
    "It is customary," John explained, "for us to sponsor a kinsmen or
a friend, if they are in need and we have a little extra to give. When I
returned home to find my family dead and my house invaded by adver-

saries, my sponsor—an army general, who assisted me in Uganda—helped me to get back on my feet. Now that I am surviving okay, I have become Habimana's sponsor. I told the store owner that I am Habimana's sponsor, and if he comes into the store for food or supplies, the owner can just keep a record of his purchases and I will pay when I come back from my work travels. My little bit of generosity," John said proudly, "has even helped his daughter go to school."

This is just a small, but illustrative, example of a philanthropy model that I have seen in many developing countries. Unlike Western philanthropy toward strangers (usually aimed at social or environmental "causes"), some Africans and Asians engage in *favoritism philanthropy*. In Asia I have seen many cases of prosperous or middle-class men and women acting as sponsors or mentors to favorite protégés—smoothing their way in life, with proper introductions, money, skills education, sometimes housing, and general aid.

We have some cultural practices like this in the West. One thinks of the highly supportive role of godparents, for example, in some families. But sponsorship in the developing world is a much bigger part of the ethical and social culture. Affection is the glue that binds the giver and the receiver in this model of charity. Emotions like *care*, not moral *principles*, motivate these personal ethical stories. Patronage is based on kin favoritism originally, but it has evolved into a broader social system that goes beyond blood. Nonetheless, "brotherhood" and other filial metaphors are frequently on the lips of Africans, when they talk about wider issues of politics. Like many Africans, it is through the lens of patrons and protégés that my Rwandan friend sees the bigger political drama.

He didn't speak of fairness, the evils of nepotism, blind justice, or any of the egalitarian principles that we trumpet in the West. He wanted to know, instead, why some leaders would not share more of their wealth with their less fortunate "brothers." The lack of *care* that Congo rulers had for their own people infuriated him, for example.

"How can the rulers in Congo grow rich on diamonds, but fail to build a single paved road in the whole country?" he asked me, in helpless outrage.

"The richer African countries," he continued, "should be sponsors, and help their poor brothers in other African countries. They should not run off to 'parties'—abandoning their own families." Finally, looking out the window of his truck, he said, in exasperation but almost dreamily, "This was supposed to be our time."

I close with this discussion to show how an alternative ethics of sponsorship (triggered and sustained by the *care* of favoritism) can inspire the microcosm of village life and the macrocosm of national politics in places like Africa and Asia. It would be a misinterpretation of my Rwanda example to see John's wistfulness as a condemnation of patronage ethics. Africa is still too close, historically speaking, to its painful emergence from colonialism (and subsequent civil wars) to know if the favoritism model of benevolence will thrive and produce progress. The patronage model (and, of course, new economics) has certainly served China well. I am optimistic that John will get his dream one day, but it won't be because Africans gave up patronage and accepted the grid of impartiality. You don't root out corruption by breaking nepotism and tribalism. You root out kleptocracy by re-educating people who confuse *materialism* and *wealth* with *happiness* and *success*. You reduce corruption by reducing greed. That kind of reeducation is needed as much in the West as it is in the developing world.

6

"Your People Shall Be My People?"

The title of this chapter adds a question mark to the famous line from the book of Ruth from the Old Testament of the Bible. The new punctuation invites us to wonder about transcending tribe. How capacious can we make our tribes? Ruth is a Moabite woman who marries the Israelite Naomi's son. Moabite people and Israelites are distant relations anyway, but the cultural differences are still large and the story invites us to consider the expansions of kin loyalty. When Naomi's son dies, she releases Ruth from the obligation of staying with the family she married into, allowing here to return to her own biological family. But Ruth refuses to go and stays loyal to Naomi, saying, "Do not urge me to leave you. . . . For where you will go I will go, and where you lodge I will lodge. Your people shall be my people, and your God my God" (Ruth 1:16).

The story shows us a flexible devotion—one that can refasten onto a new tribe and extend all the preferential treatments. Ruth displays heroic loyalty to her new tribe and is rewarded later in life with prosperity and reputation (she is a great-grandmother of David). The story

Fig. 18. The biblical story of Ruth is a meditation on loyalty and the bounds of filial
allegiance. Here Ruth pledges her devotion to her mother-in-law, Naomi.
Drawing by Stephen Asma, based on medieval representations.

looks at first like a lesson in inclusivity, a lesson in unity across tribal
divides. But closer examination complicates the moral. First, Ruth's
people and Naomi's people are not that different. They share a common ancestor in Terah, the grandfather of Lot, who fled Sodom and
Gomorrah (Genesis 19:37). Second, most Jewish interpretations of
the story underscore the singular importance of Ruth's conversion to
Naomi's God. Ruth attains favor by converting to Judaism. Her blood
tribe is replaced or substituted with a religious tribe, Judaism. The
story is certainly not one of universal liberal inclusion. Ruth flourishes
because she joins the right clan, so to speak. The God of the Old Testament plays favorites—he clearly has a chosen people, and they in turn
acknowledge and honor their favored status.

Being Jewish, even today, is a tribal issue. To be a Jew is to be a member of an ethno-religious group, usually by birth but also by conversion. Of course, the relationship between ethnic and religious identity is fuzzy in Judaism. Allegiance to Jewish law is crucial for some notions of identity, but being born of a Jewish mother is automatic membership according to other criteria.[1] A debate simmered in the twentieth century as to whether modern Diaspora Jews are blood-related back to the time of the biblical exodus, or whether different groups are descended from *converted* non-blood-related populations. Recent genetic analysis seems to favor the blood-relation hypothesis because DNA of diverse Jewish groups shows striking continuity and common descent.[2] But the point for us is not "Who is a Jew?" in the ontological sense, but "What are your loyalty values if you see yourself as Jewish?" Or if you view yourself as black? Or as Irish? Or lesbian? Or Democrat?

Do many Jewish people privilege their tribe over the interests of non-Jews? Of course they do, and why shouldn't they? Tribal favoritism is even more justified when your tribe is under siege, as in the

Fig. 19. Judaism sees the Jews as the chosen people (or the treasured people) of Yahweh. Religious solidarity and ethnocentrism are common forms or favoritism down through the ages. Here Moses accepts the Ten Commandments. Drawing by Stephen Asma, based on Marc Chagall's *Moses* (1966).

case of centuries of Diaspora anti-Semitism. Lip service to universal brotherhood is all fine and good, but not when it's accompanied by pogroms and persecutions.

This chapter will investigate the complex relationship between favoritism within in-groups and larger social contexts. Are there *limits* to our kin circles and our favoritism circles, or can we expand them indefinitely until we all become one tribe?

Minorities, Majorities, and Favoritism

The reader will have noticed that I've said very little so far about gender and race. It's not because I forgot. In fact, it's striking that I've been able to cover so much territory in a book about fairness and not get to gender and race until now. This has been by design. If I had started in that familiar place, we would never have traversed the other expansive territories of bias and favoritism. The bigger philosophical conversation cannot unfold if we begin with the usual hot-button issues.

Since fairness is the paradigm language that Americans use to talk about civil rights equality and the women's movement, any doubts about fairness are automatically perceived as backward and prejudiced. This is because emotions, understandably, mix up the issues. By now, however, the reader appreciates how justice and the good are much bigger realities than simple fairness, so it is possible to critique fairness while preserving liberal social justice. This is not just a logical point.

There is a kind of secret history of the civil rights and feminist movements that doesn't fit with the official egalitarian version. Feelings of tribal favoritism (in-group affiliation of minority groups) played as much a role as any principle of equality in demanding a place at the table (where other tribes were already feeding). Political empowerment movements are effective because a tribe (in this case racial or gender specific) gets powerful enough to no longer be ignored. My view of American history is that progress always comes by this contest of groups, not by some implementation of abstract egalitarian principles. The dubious official history that we're taught about rights movements is that minority groups recognized the *hypocrisy* in majority group conduct and policy, and demanded that they align their aberrant behaviors with their formal grid of egalitarianism. Don't just talk the talk of egalitarian fairness, walk the walk. As a neat revision of historical progress, this version plays well—placing oppressed minorities in the position of moral heroes and the majority is cast as hypocritical villains.

The cultural take-away from this dubious history has been interesting. Liberals often interpret this to mean that minority groups, subalterns, and oppressed people are more egalitarian—more authentically fair—than the corrupted majority.[3] Minorities, it is suggested, have held the majority's feet to the flames of equality, finally forcing them to live by their own principles. This naive story is perfectly fine as part of our idealistic national myth, but it only helps to obscure the realities of human favoritism by whitewashing them with a pious narrative about the triumph of fairness.

Minority groups are not *less* biased, nepotistic, partial, or "favoritist" than the majority. On the contrary, they are splendidly *more* so. It is demonstrably absurd to think of minority groups as pockets of egalitarian fairness, struggling to chastise the nepotistic majority into like-minded morality.

Anyone whose family are recent immigrants to the United States is familiar with the traditions of positive nepotism. My hometown of Chicago is built on ethnic neighborhoods, centers for the communication of talent, money, labor, and opportunity between the old world and the new. Whether it's Chinese people following the First Transcontinental Railway to Chicago in the late nineteenth century, Back-of-the-Yards Polish, or contemporary Mexicans in Pilsen; the city is not so much a melting pot as a bento box of tribal groups. And of course the whole country, not just Chicago, is built on this unique influx of diverse ethnicity. But if your people and your family came to the States ages ago, you may feel little or no tribal affiliation (in the ethnic sense). If your parents or grandparents are still speaking a mother tongue, however, then chances are you feel the sway of clan quite keenly.

Strict egalitarianism teaches us to ignore ethnicity, race, and gender, and of course in some domains—like equality before the law—this ideal is exactly right. Unfortunately, overemphasis on fairness has led us to think that *all* domains of life must be color-blind in order for them to be ethical. The immigrant, however, teaches us a different lesson—the lesson of virtuous preferential treatment.

Immigrant populations in the United States can be great examples of generosity, loyalty, devotion, and the pursuit of excellence. But this ethical treasure is uniquely bounded inside the circle of ethnic favorites, not spread indiscriminately to the mainstream. We don't have to go all the way to China or India, as we did in chapter 5, to see the cultures of ethical favoritism in action. Immigrant Italians, Mexicans, Jews, Chinese, Africans, and so on practice favoritism in very successful ways—ways that are not simply dismissible as necessary survival techniques (though they certainly do help with survival in a foreign land).

Successful immigrant networking systems are rooted in blood tribalism, expanding out from nuclear to extended family, then out to village, then out to ethnicity. Wealth, even modest wealth, is concentrated and transferred between family members who are separated by miles, even oceans. Family helps family, and ethnic group members help group members.

Work is one of the main areas where tribal networking pays off, and pockets of preferential hiring flourish under the radar of official business. Workers who share a common heritage will help each other secure employment, and managers will often preferentially hire workers of a similar heritage. It is impolite in our official culture to point out the obvious ethnic affiliations that fill many of our workplaces, but only willful ignorance can hide the facts. I worked in an office where an African American woman became manager, and within a year the complexion of the staff was transformed. Almost every new hire, from clerks to custodians was black. And I've witnessed the same workplace transformation along the lines of sexual orientation. As usual, I am not against such preferential hiring per se, unless the practice is immoderate and excessive.

In Chicago, Mexican immigration is strong, and the bonds between hometown compatriots create networks of mutual assistance and support. I asked Jacqueline Herrera-Giron, an immigration lawyer in Lake

County, Illinois, to explain some positive forms of favoritism in immigrant populations.

"Many of the Mexicans that you find in Chicago," Herrera-Giron told me, "come from a specific region of Mexico—the state of Michoacán. There is a strong bond that ties the newer immigrant population with the older homeland. In many cases, grandparents may remain in the old country, and parents, siblings, cousins, and friends can all be separated geographically. But of course immigrants send money back to the family in Mexico."

It's as if a niche from Mexico buds off and creates a new niche in Chicago, with strong transnational, translocal connectivity. Herrera-Giron, who is from El Salvador and whose husband is from Guatemala, explains that many U.S. immigrant populations thrive because wisdom and wealth is shared in tight networked systems that cross national borders. Herrera-Giron works north of Chicago in Waukegan, Illinois, where the Mexican population originates almost entirely from a little Mexican town in Michoacán called La Luz. Every January 12, Waukegan immigrants return to La Luz, where the tiny plaza explodes with a dollar-fueled celebration. Families, dressed in their finest, reunite, and resources are shared generously among kin and friends.

"Many immigrants pool resources," Herrera-Giron explained, "to buy the eldest sibling a house. Then, once that is achieved, they start to pool wealth to buy the next sibling a house, and so on. But this kind of help extends, in lesser forms, to compatriots too. There are, for example, 'Home Town Federations'—social groups that do fund-raising and send money back to Mexico. These are made up of family, friends, and neighbors.

"In La Luz," Herrera-Giron continued, "there was no running water or electricity until the Waukegan Home Town Federation channeled money down to modernize the city. Now these federations—that exist all over the U.S.—are actually evolving into political groups that have growing political influence in both countries."

None of this success—spread out over two nations—would be possible if it wasn't for a network of nepotistic favoritism in everything from transportation, to marriage, to employment, to politics. There is tremendous generosity, diligence, perseverance, and ethical selfless-ness in these networks, but they are insider systems. They don't extend to strangers. And these allegiances frequently follow ethnic lines as well as family lines. When I explained to Herrera-Giron that Chinese people rarely give money or resources to strangers (always privileging family instead), she agreed that this was the value system in her own El Salvadoran family. "The idea of giving money to strangers seems foreign to me," she confessed, "but maybe this is because I'm [a] first-generation immigrant. Survival often means a strong network of fam-ily resources."

What is the relationship of minorities and majorities in the real world of favoritism? Ethnic and gender solidarity is not always to the disad-vantage of others, but sometimes it is, and we need to think about a workable system of social justice beyond the utopian thought experi-ments of disinterested egalitarianism.

In California a federal judge struck down a ban on gay marriage in 2010. In 2011 it was discovered that the judge was actually in a long-term same-sex relationship himself, and so the opponents of gay mar-riage cried foul, arguing that the judge, Vaughn Walker, was biased and partial, because his ruling in favor of gay marriage might advan-tage his own situation. Opponents of gay marriage argued that there was a conflict-of-interest bias.

Defenders of Vaughn Walker and gay marriage made the only kind of rhetorical response available in official circles. "There is absolutely not one scintilla of evidence that . . . who [Walker] is biased him against the proponents [of the ban]," said Kate Kendell, executive director of the National Center for Lesbian Rights.[4] The defense of Judge Walker followed the usual egalitarian lines of idealism: Walker was totally un-biased; heterosexuals can be impartial about gays, and gays can be impartial about heteros; white judges can be impartial about blacks, and blacks can be impartial about whites; men can be impartial about women, and women about men; and so on. Defenders of Walker sug-gested that he was like a blindfolded Lord Justice—able to divest from all his own interests and then adjudicate from the abstract Rawlsian space of utter neutrality.

I see no reason to join this sanctimonious choir of idealism. My argument has made space for another view, besides nemocentric fairness. In this case, I am in praise of both Walker's biased judgment and the liberal cause at stake—the inclusion of gays in the institution of marriage. But there is no need to deny the former to attain the latter.

If we really believed in the impartial neutrality of judges (and human beings generally), then we wouldn't work to increase the ethnic and gender diversity of judges. I have no problem thinking the gay judge was biased, but I would argue that this was a good thing. His affiliation with gays makes him sensitive to subtle jurisprudence issues that heterosexual judges may miss; it makes him a defender of a "tribe" that has been unjustly treated; it helps him educate his constituency; it helps him (should such cases arise) direct medical research to diseases like HIV/AIDS; it helps him empower his community.

Many women were drawn to Hillary Clinton's presidential campaign, for example, because she was a woman and would explicitly and implicitly put women's issues into a preferential position—a position that they have not previously enjoyed. I support this example of tribal favoritism and feel no need to dress it up with haughty appeals to impartial universal fairness. In the case of the gay judge and the female president, we see traditional liberal social causes served by illiberal tribal realities. And while this might be ironic, it's not really irrational or unethical.

Supreme Court Justice Sonia Sotomayor almost failed to get confirmed in 2009 because she had the nerve (or naïveté) to state, in an earlier speech, an obvious fact: a Latina may be in a better position to empathize with non-whites who come before her bench. She claimed in a 2001 speech that her minority status helped her to better empathize with people in her courtroom. Her *affiliation*, in other words—not her nemocentrism—helped her to be a better judge. This claim was quickly twisted around by political enemies to mean that Sotomayor was racist against whites. She had apparently sinned against the facade of fairness neutrality.

American politics is loaded with tribalism masquerading as fairness. Liberals who supported President Obama often did so on the grounds that they were restoring fairness to an imbalanced preferential system. Obama himself argued, as part of his 2008 campaign, that he would take back Washington from the special interests, lobbyists, and patronage culture. Egalitarianism was the official rhetoric. However, in 2011 the Center for Public Integrity discovered that donors to Obama's 2008 campaign (usually "bundlers" who aggregated fundraising) were rewarded with administration jobs. Over two hundred of these supporters were given ambassadorships, policy advisor jobs, or other placements in federal agencies like the Department of Justice, the Federal Communications Commission, and so on. Consequently a new group of people has power and access to more power.

Now, my own response to this is to yawn—what could be more unsurprising?—but also to use it as an example of reasonable favoritism. I think it is fine that Obama has staffed his administration with supporters. It helps him achieve his political goals, it provides him with fresh perspective from his constituency, and it both ensures and rewards loyalty. Presidents Bush and Clinton did the same thing before Obama. In party politics the contest is always preferential and tribal, but it is amusing to watch liberals deny their own tribalism. When the other guy has power, it is unfair cronyism. But when you yourself have power, it is disinterested egalitarian justice.

Affirmative Action and Favoritism

The lingo of fairness has obscured a more interesting conversation about favoritism and group interaction—how *do* and how *should* the many contesting tribal groups fraternize? This is especially pressing in pluralistic societies like the United States. Many theorists debate whether the assimilation (melting-pot) model or the multiculturalism (bento-box) model fits best with the American egalitarian ideology. The melting-pot model celebrates the universal transcultural *similarities* of different groups, and the multiculturalism model celebrates the uniquely cultural *differences* between groups. I suspect that the melting-pot model is more resonant with egalitarian ideology, but since I'm not a big fan of that ideology, I tend to lean the other way. Without getting too mired in that debate, I should just situate my own pro-tribal view as more in tune with the multicultural position—in the sense that real social identity comes most strongly from very *local* bonds, rather than abstract universals. I recognize, of course, that tribal affiliation is a fluid and flexible relation. A Bostonian might feel very *Catholic* while visiting his Protestant friend in Alabama, and the two of them might feel very *American* when they visit their atheist friend in Paris, but all three of them might feel very *Western* when they take a trip to Vietnam. While this flexibility of affiliation is uncontroversial, my argument has been that *affection* or *emotion* is the glue of true tribal fidelity, and this places serious constraints on the expansion of favoritism. For example, even in cases where soldiers appear to fight and die for huge abstract tribes like "America," further examination reveals the very *local* heart of their real motivation—the parents back home, the sweetheart, the newborn daughter, the little bungalow neighborhood, and so on. Laura Hillenbrand's book *Unbroken* gives us a glimpse into the local bonds of affection that fueled World War II American soldiers as they fought overseas—or in the case of Louis Zamperini (the subject of *Unbroken*), as they languished in prisoner of war camps. "On an October afternoon, Louie stepped out of an army car and stood on the lawn at 2028 Gramercy Avenue, looking at his parents' house for the first time in more than three years. 'This, this little home,' he said, 'was worth all of it.'"

How should we view "affirmative action" after my rejection of the utopian grid of impartiality? Is my demotion of fairness, and promotion of favoritism, consonant with affirmative action? Are preferential hiring and education admissions cases of favoritism—and if so, do they create more equality and fairness or undermine these goals? And if they undermine egalitarian fairness, are they still defensible in a broader context of social ethics?

President Lyndon B. Johnson signed Executive Order 11246, requiring equal employment opportunity, in 1965. It was aimed at governmental contractors, preventing them from discriminating along lines of "race, color, religion, sex, or national origin." And it ordered contractors to "take affirmative action to ensure that applicants are employed, and that employees are treated during employment, without regard to their race, color, religion, sex, or national origin." Shortly

Fig. 20. The architects of affirmative action, Lyndon B. Johnson (1908–1973) and
John F. Kennedy (1917–1963). Drawing by Stephen Asma.

after Johnson's order, colleges and universities nationwide began to
adopt affirmative action. In a commencement speech that Johnson
delivered at Howard University in 1965, he said, "You do not take a
person who, for years, has been hobbled by chains and liberate him,
bring him up to the starting line of a race and then say, 'you are free to
compete with all the others,' and still justly believe that you have been
completely fair."[5]

Affirmative action seeks to ensure access to minorities who have
been victims, historically, of discrimination. African Americans, for
example, were profoundly disadvantaged by slavery and subsequent
Jim Crow laws. Affirmative action introduced the restorative policy
dictating that if two candidates come to a job interview (or university
admission) with equal skills, the minority candidate should take pre-
cedence. But the policy often went further, preferring members of historically disadvantaged groups even when the representative persons

were less skilled than other applicants. This was done on the grounds, purportedly, that such handicapping would eventually balance out the current lack of an even playing field.

The irony of what happened next is similar to the legal development of anti-nepotism policies that we looked at in the previous chapter. The Equal Protection Clause of the Fourteenth Amendment, which was originally used to create affirmative action, was now used *against* subsequent applications of the policy. People who were bumped from schools and jobs because of an affirmative action program brought their own Equal Protection claims, challenging the constitutionality of the program—saying that since the basis of the discriminatory program (the affirmative action program) is race (because it let in blacks, for example, and it discriminated against the white challenger), *strict scrutiny* applies.[6] What does this mean?

Strict scrutiny is a part of a three-criteria standard of review—a set of conditions that justify an Equal Protection action. In short, the countersuits could not change the constitutionality of affirmative action (nothing short of a constitutional amendment can do that), but they created a much more onerous justification for exercising the program (it became much more difficult to argue a compelling state interest without explicit proof of past discrimination in the specific institution in question). This strict scrutiny has radically reduced the number of affirmative action cases in the courts today.

In the context of public universities, then, we have seen a rolling back of affirmative action policies. This is somewhat predictable because the new burdensome standards of review apply to Equal Protection, and Equal Protection claims are leveled against the government, not the private sector. The law may bar discrimination in the private sphere on the basis of other rationales (e.g., the Commerce Clause, which was useful in the passage of Civil Rights legislation), but Equal Protection claims don't apply. State schools are now free to take a laissez-faire approach to affirmative action, while many private schools are trying to sustain the preferential admission policies that ensure campus diversity.

Some states like Michigan have even recently passed constitutional amendments that prohibit state agencies from operating affirmative action programs. When California did this a decade ago, it had swift and dramatic repercussions for university admissions. "Within little less than a decade, black enrollment in the freshman class at UCLA had dropped from 211 to 96 and at UC Berkeley from 258 to 140."[7] This is because the Scholastic Aptitude Test scores are very uneven when considered along ethnic demographics. Asians and whites score about the same in reading and writing, while Asians (581 points) rocket ahead in math (whites score 537). Mexican Americans score around 75–130 points below whites and Asians, and black students trail Mexican Americans by 20–40 points in all categories. The causes of these discrepancies are complex and need economic, political, and cultural solutions. But one thing is clear. If test-score merit alone became the criteria for American universities, then institutions of higher learning would quickly become overwhelmingly white and Asian—and probably, before too long, overwhelmingly Asian.

When President Johnson first instituted affirmative action, one of the underlying purposes was reparation to the descendants of former slaves. African Americans who felt the sting of racism directly were helped by the policy. The goal of increased diversity, in schools and the workplace, was intimately connected to this reparation function of affirmative action, but that is no longer the case. In today's America, many of the people who benefit from diversity policies are not disadvantaged African Americans, but Latinos, Indians, Africans, Vietnamese, Iranians, Pakistanis, Chinese, Koreans, and so on. Nowadays there is tremendous diversity on university campuses, so critics of affirmative action feel comfortable calling for termination of the policy. Many people argue that the policy has successfully balanced a previous imbalance (lack of diversity), and so what was once a *fair preference* has now evolved into an *unfair preference*.[8]

Add to this perspective the argument by middle- and upper-class African Americans that we've outgrown affirmative action, and we see the policy slipping away in contemporary political conversation. President Obama, for example, has stated that his own privileged daughters don't deserve affirmative action preferences.[9] Instead, he argues, low-income students of all races should be given preferential treatment. At the same time, his own Department of Justice supported race-based admissions at a recent University of Texas case.[10]

Suffice it to say, there is not only significant confusion around the role of affirmative action in our egalitarian culture, but also conflicting intuitions (in the same individual) about its role in the good society. A simple appeal to fairness does not help, since meritocratic rejection of the policy looks perfectly fair in correlating the skills of students with their deserts. But then again, preferential admittance also looks fair in the real world of imbalanced playing fields.[11]

We also have a different complexion in the United States these days—different from when preferential racial policies first emerged. Not only is there more diverse immigrant color in the tribes of contemporary America, but also a new generation (or two) of racially mixed offspring. The intermediary shades—the two-tribe offspring, like my own son—are growing rapidly. When it comes to schools and other opportunities, I play the odds—like every other parent of mixed-race kids. If I can give him some advantage by marking him as "Chinese" on some application, I do it. If there seems an advantage to being marked white, I do it. Both designations are true, after all. The trouble in these days of quota lotteries and handicapping is that it is nigh impossible to figure out which racial designation will help and which will harm. If a school thinks there are too many whites admitted, then some minority status will be helpful for admittance. But Asian applicants frequently outperform other candidates and have to be discriminated *against* to keep them from overpopulating competitive programs.[12]

Massaging institutional systems to the advantage of your own tribe is, of course, an old and ubiquitous story. Economist Thomas Sowell argues, however, that the history of affirmative action policies in India, Sri Lanka, Nigeria, and Malaysia reveals a series of worrisome consequences.[13] First, affirmative action encourages non-preferred groups and individuals to redesignate themselves as preferred (victim) groups, in order to take advantage of the preferred group policies. Secondly, Sowell—himself African American—claims that affirmative action policies often benefit the most fortunate of the preferred group (e.g., wealthy people of color) rather than the less fortunate. And Sowell also argues that such policies reduce incentives for both preferred and non-preferred groups to do their best. Preferred groups don't have to work hard, according to Sowell, and non-preferred groups will not be rewarded when they do.

Those who oppose affirmative action usually do so on the grounds that it goes beyond mere equal opportunity and thereby spoils our merit-based systems of excellence. Conservatives and libertarians rely on the notion of fairness that says: Merit deserves more. And of course this merit-based fairness vies against the liberal notion of fairness as "equal shares" or "equal outcomes." My idea of tribal favoritism, as a unit of ethical value and action, comes to this old two-party fight like a prickly independent. Where do my allegiance circles of favoritism fit in this fight over fairness?

First, it's important to point out, as I've done repeatedly throughout this book, that fairness—even as an ideal—is not robust enough to handle our big ethical challenges. It's like bringing an accountant, armed with a ledger, to the front lines of a war zone, asking him to sort out the trouble. Larger moral frameworks, like the good of the commonwealth, are more helpful than egalitarian grids. Understanding the moral health of the nation, for example, is not all that different from understanding the health of an individual. As I discussed in chapter 3, understanding and solving moral problems is similar to a physician taking a medical history (with all the idiosyncrasies, anomalies, and exceptions). When we switch from the egalitarian grid to this unique, historically sensitive approach, we find room for harm-reduction responses to troubled organs in the social body.

Using this approach of commonwealth good, we can recognize that some groups have been disadvantaged by historical abuses and need remedial measures. This is not a question of fairness or even equality per se, but the health and well-being of the social organism. To continue my medical analogy, if I have been abusing my lower back at work for years, then my vertebral alignment may become compromised, my other back muscles may try to overcompensate and become damaged, my hip may go out, and my ability to walk and work might unravel.

Is it that much different to point out that a social group—having been abused for many years—can become the catalyst for a cascade of social ills, if we fail to pursue healthy amelioration? Helping people get educations and jobs, for example, also reduces crime, just like helping people improve fitness also reduces health care costs. In our analogy, it will probably be good for the lower back and eventually the whole body if new strengthening exercises and greater burden is placed temporarily on the stomach muscles. "No fair!" cry the stomach muscles. "Get over it," responds the physician. Fairness is not the point.[14] And notice, after our dismissal of the fairness criterion, that we are *not* left mute or helpless when trying to harmonize the competing tribal interests of biological and social bodies.

So, then, how do we evaluate affirmative action after we've stopped trying to force it into an unnatural fit with egalitarian philosophy? First, let's respond to the criticism that such policies lead non-preferred groups and individuals to redesignate themselves as preferred (victim) groups, in order to take advantage of the preferred group policies. Well, to be frank, I fail to see the problem here. Yes, I will try to get my son designated as Chinese if it bestows some advantage on him—white if that works better, maybe even Latino if I can figure out how to do it. I'll also try to make him *tall* (by stuffing him with nutritious food), and later in life he may choose to wear thick-heeled shoes to "redesignate" himself as taller (and thereby attain significant advantages). Some people try to redesignate themselves as *attractive* (by means both cosmetic and surgical), and many people try to get others to categorize them as *smart* (sometimes a preferred group) or even *dumb* (also sometimes a preferred group). Still others will use slightly different versions of their names, or even rename themselves, when they perceive that certain ethnic names will get preference. The only moral jeopardy I see here is possible deception, but there are myriad forms of changeable identity representation that do not constitute fraud. More importantly, my argument has consistently placed the ethics of family loyalty over universal maxims (whether biblical or Kantian), so even lying to strangers to advantage kin is not a major sin in my book.

What about the criticism that affirmative action policies often benefit the most fortunate of the preferred group (e.g., wealthy people of color) rather than the less fortunate? Here is a situation where history matters, in our physician case-history approach to social ethics. If race-based preferences were healthy in the early days of affirmative action, but they're now failing to reach the truly disadvantaged, then it's time to retool the policy along the lines of *class* rather than *race*. When our black president tells us that the time has come to shift preferences from race to class, we should take the suggestion seriously.

Lastly, how do we respond to the criticism that preferential policies reduce incentives for both preferred and non-preferred groups to do their best? People won't work hard if they get handouts, according to Thomas Sowell. Like other free-market proselytizers, Sowell assumes that there is some higher good above the level of citizen happiness—something like nation-state status—and that this geopolitical status (as innovators, world leaders, with technological or economic superiority) trumps any happiness and prosperity of its welfare citizenry (who will, supposedly, grow fat and lazy as lotus eaters). This might be true, though I doubt it.

My ongoing emphasis on small, local, tribal units means that "success" is measured on the kith-and-kin stage, not the geopolitical stage. If *my people* are sufficiently satisfied, safe, and happy (a difficult accomplishment), then my work/career ambitions might well wane, but so what? For the favoritist, the meaning of life—if I can use so grandiose a term—comes much closer to hand than the geopolitical or the cosmic drama. When many free-market proselytizers speak of meritocracy, they have a narrow concept of excellence in mind. They tend to equate excellence with economic success, and fail to factor in the broader pursuits of excellence—in artistic, spiritual, athletic domains.

Let's take Sowell's worst fear as realized. Let's say that my job came to me from preferential treatment, and this fact leads me to do mediocre work. Okay. But I am more than my job. We are all *more than* our jobs. Worker productivity is not the best measure of human excellence, and the goal of social policy is not to protect entrepreneurial gumption at all costs. When Chinese garment workers immigrated to the little Italian town of Prato, in Tuscany, they radically increased the speed and volume of textile production in the region. They also ate and slept in their workplaces, where they often labored for eighteen hours a day. The Chinese did *not* share in the indigenous Italian tradition of "siesta culture"—taking off work for several hours in the afternoon to eat, rest, and enjoy family. Yes, Chinese productivity outstripped the local Italians, but something precious was lost. Profits went up, but humanity did not. Give me siesta life any day, not because I'm lazy but because life is more than work.

Some preferential policies give people access to education and work that would otherwise not happen. This is good for the minority individual and group because it improves their lives, and good for the majority group because it injects fresh insights, perspectives, traditions, and skills into the community, and raises the level of educated citizenry (and it also reduces crime).[15] Using the broader notion of commonwealth health, then, we can see that "decreased productivity" (should it result) is not some intrinsic or inherent sin. It is only a strike against preferential policies if we start the evaluation with an overly narrow measure of human "success."

The Finite Stretch

How far can we stretch our allegiance? Can we overcome factionalism and eventually become one giant tribe? Two of the leading liberal social theorists, Jeremy Rifkin and Peter Singer, think we can. I think they're wrong.

Recall that we met Peter Singer, the utilitarian philosopher, in chapter 2, because his view that everyone possesses the same value and importance did not jibe very well with our intuitions about moral gravity. A brief return to his view is relevant in this section on tribal expansion, because he has been very influential in arguing for transcending tribalism.

In his book *The Expanding Circle*, Singer argues that social evolution required our ancestors to make group decisions in order to survive, but internal disputes were inevitable. After the rise of language-slinging big brains, group members solved their disputes by offering reasons—justifications that appealed to the interests of others. These rudimentary considerations of others' interests scaffolded upward, over time, to create group-oriented interests above and beyond individual interests. With increased neocortical sophistication, humans can now, according to Singer, rationally broaden their ethical duty beyond the tribe to an equal and impartial concern for all human beings.

"If I have seen," Singer writes, "that from an ethical point of view I am just one person among the many in my society, and my interests are no more important, from the point of view of the whole, than the similar interests of others within my society, I am ready to see that, from a still larger point of view, my society is just one among other societies, and the interests of members of my society are no more important, from that larger perspective, than the similar interests of members of other societies." Like mathematics, which can continue its recursive operations infinitely upward, ethical reasoning can spiral out (*should* spiral out, according to Singer) to larger and larger sets of equal moral subjects. "Taking the impartial element in ethical reasoning to its logical conclusion means, first, accepting that we ought to have equal concern for all human beings."[16]

All this sounds nice at first, but ultimately rings hollow. Singer seems to be suggesting that I arrive at perfect egalitarian ethics by first accepting perfect egalitarian metaphysics. But I, for one, do not accept it. Nor, I venture to guess, do many others. People are not equally entitled to my time, affection, resources, or moral duties—and only a naive imagination can make them appear so. It seems dubious to say that we should transcend tribe and be utilitarian because all people are equal, when the equal status of strangers and kin is an unproven and counterintuitive assumption. Singer voices the basic egalitarian starting place when he says, "If I have seen that from an ethical point of view I am just one person among the many in my society, and my interests are no more important . . . than the similar interests of others within my society."[17] But that is a very big "if." I will even go so far as to say that *no one*, unless they are trying to impress someone in cocktail chatter, will wholly get on board with that "if."

Singer's abstract "ethical point of view" is not wrong so much as irrelevant. Yes, from space, orbiting the planet, all our interests look equal, but we're not living there. I don't look down from the top of the

John Hancock building in Chicago, notice that everyone below looks like bugs, and then resolve to treat everyone like bugs ever after.

In addition, critics have persuasively gone after the principles and practices of such utilitarian ethics, particularly Singer's idea that we should do everything within our power to help strangers meet their basic needs, even if it severely compromises our kin's happiness.[18] In the calculus, needs always trump enjoyments. Without any tribal allegiance of favorites, I owe everybody the same. So, if I am to be utterly impartial to all human beings, then I should reduce my own family's life to a subsistence level, just above the poverty line, and distribute the surplus wealth to needy strangers.

Besides the impracticalities of such utopian redistribution, the problems here are also conceptual. I bought a fancy pair of shoes for my son. But in light of the one-tribe calculus of interests, I should probably give these shoes to someone who doesn't have any. I do research and find a kid in Cambodia who needs shoes to walk to school every day. So, I take them off my son (replacing them with Walmart tennis shoes) and head off to the post office to send the shoes to the Cambodia kid. On the way, I see a newspaper story about five kids who are malnourished. Now, I can't give Cambodia kid the shoes, because I should sell the shoes for money and use the money to get food for the five malnourished kids. On my way to sell the shoes, I remember that my son has an important job interview for a clean-water nonprofit NGO, and if he gets the job, he'll be able to help save whole villages from contaminated water. But he won't get the job if he shows up in Walmart tennis shoes. As I head back home, it dawns on me that for many people in the developing world, Walmart tennis shoes are truly *luxurious* when compared with burlap sack shoes, and since needs always trump luxuries I'll need to sell the tennis shoes too; and on, and on, and on.

In addition to the dizzying and contradictory nature of these rapidly multiplying one-tribe "obligations," it is important to notice something else. All this philanthropy itself starts to look like a luxury, a surplus of goodwill and energy. Many people can't do a fraction of these good deeds for strangers, because they're literally too busy and exhausted from taking care of their own small family. Many Americans live paycheck to paycheck and constantly hustle one gig after another so they can pay for groceries, lodging, and the rare cultural indulgence like piano lessons for their kid. Those people who do a lot of philanthropy can afford to do it. And I don't mean just financially.

The "saints of the leisured class," as I'll call them, are drawn from the ranks of people who can pay their bills, send their kids to the best private schools, vacation in exotic lands, stay out of debt, and shop at Whole Foods. But the other great surplus—far less conspicuous than finances—is care. Can you have a surplus of empathy?

This brings us to the other recent argument for transcending tribe, and it's the idea that we can infinitely stretch our domain of care. Jeremy Rifkin voices a popular view, in his recent book *The Empathic Civilization*, that we can *feel* care and empathy for the whole human species if we just try hard enough.[19] This neo-hippie view has the advantage over Singer's metric view, in that it locates moral conviction in the heart rather than the rational head. But it fails for another reason.

I submit that care or empathy is a limited resource. But the neo-hippie view is that empathy is a limitless reserve. Rifkin sketches a progressive, ever-widening, evolution of empathy. First, we had blood-based tribalism, then religion-based tribalism, then nation-state tribalism, but now we are poised for an empathic embrace of all humanity—and even beyond species-centric bias to Buddha-like compassion for all creatures. He argues that empathy is the real "invisible hand" that will guide us out of our local and global crises.

Using a secular version of Gandhi's non-attachment mixed with some old-fashioned apocalyptic fearmongering, Rifkin warns us that we must reach "biosphere consciousness and global empathy in time to avert planetary collapse."[20] The way to do this is to start feeling as if the entire human race is our extended family.

Now, in some abstract sense, I agree with the idea of an evolutionary shared descent that makes us all "family." But feelings of care and empathy are very different from evolutionary taxonomy. As we saw extensively in chapter 2, empathy is a biological emotion that comes in degrees, because it has a specific physiological chemical process. Empathy is not a concept, but a natural biological event—an activity, a process. The feeling of care is triggered by a perception or internal awareness and soon swells, flooding the brain and body with subjective feelings and behaviors. Care is like sprint racing. It takes time—duration through time, energy, systemic warm-up and cooldown, practice, and a strange mixture of pleasure and pain (attraction and repulsion). Like sprinting, it's not the kind of thing you can do all the time. You will literally break the system in short order, if you ramp up the care system every time you see someone in need. The nightly news would render you literally exhausted. The limbic system can't handle the kind of constant stimulation that Rifkin and the neo-hippies expect of it. And that's because they don't understand the biology of empathy, and imagine instead that care is more like a *thought*—flitting effortlessly through the mind.

Even in the more flexible higher brain, care is a limited resource. Biologist Robin Dunbar argues that our big neocortex evolved in connection with our ability to manage increasingly bigger social tribes. Our ancestors had to keep careful track not just of mom, dad, and siblings, but also who was a friend and foe, who was a peer, who was a cousin, who was a hothead, who was a soothing presence, who was a freeloader, who shared food, and so on. Dunbar argues that the number of people that humans can reasonably engage with is around 150.[21] More than that and you start to get highly unstable, unsuccessful networks of people. One hundred fifty is the limit of stable social networks because our cognitive capacities max out above that number of variables.

Significant empirical research informs Dunbar's number and confirms that most of us have around 150 acquaintances, with around ten to fifteen much closer friends, and three to five intimate friends. Moreover, Dunbar shows that the circle of friendship intimacy is quite fluid, changeable, and susceptible to decay, but kin relationships are radically more resistant to such decay. The strength of kin bonds is much stronger.

I interpret all this as compelling evidence that care is a limited resource, something that cannot stretch indefinitely to cover the massive domain of strangers and non-human animals. Of course, when we see the suffering of strangers in the street or on television, the heartstrings vibrate naturally. We can have contagion-like feelings of sympathy when we see other beings suffering, but that is a long way from the kinds of *active preferential devotions* that we marshal for members of our respective tribes. I referred to tribes as "affective communities" back in chapter 2, and here again we're reminded of the unique emotional connection between our preferred, favorite people. There's an upper limit to our tribal emotional expansion, and that limit is a good deal lower than the "biosphere."

Feeling the Stones with Your Feet

One of the deepest assumptions in these utopian visions—be they utilitarian grids or cosmic empathy theories—is that some recipe exists for giving all competing groups what they want. When all our factional value differences are eventually organized according to some mysterious recipe, then human conflict will come to an end. From their own perspectives, communism, totalitarianism, scientism, religion, and every other idealism have made this basic assumption. Like a huge root system, feeding Western culture, the old Platonic idea that perfect harmony is out there somewhere continues to inform our thinking about values. It's buried deep in the assumptions of the Enlightenment project, which strove to reconcile cultural clashes by the light of reason.

Many Westerners assume that *if* there is a deep value divide and conflict between *cultures* like Islam and Christianity, still one day (in this life or the next) the conflicts will be mended, the harmony restored, the value tensions resolved. A similar optimism informs our view of conflicts between *perspectives* like pro-life or pro-choice, or between *people* like Israelis and Palestinians. Tribes, we hope, will lay aside their weapons and embrace each other, lions will lie down with lambs, and all "outcasts" will become "favorites."

I'm optimistic about improving conflict resolution, but not hopeful about the ultimate harmony of human values and interests. Some values and modes of life rule out other modes of life. Being a wandering Romantic artist is not compatible with being a settled family man; being a devoted nun is not compatible with being an erotic escort; being a good brother is not always compatible with being a good public servant; being a servant of Allah is not always compatible with sexual liberalism; retribution is not compatible with forgiveness; being meek is not particularly compatible with being proud.

Favoritism and egalitarianism, taken together, make a very dissonant chord. But we need to get accustomed to their discordant sound. I think the British philosopher Isaiah Berlin (1909–1997) was correct when he noticed that many of our deepest values are incompatible with one another. Berlin lost faith in the idealism of "values harmony" when he read Machiavelli and realized that the pagan values, extolled by the Italian philosopher, were indeed good but still incompatible with Christian values.[22] Two competing goods (virtue systems) were forever at odds. Pride, strength, justice, and honor (classical or pagan virtues) are contradicted by humility, meekness, forgiveness, and submission. This fundamental discordance of two obviously good virtue systems led Berlin to give up Enlightenment optimism and embrace the irreconcilability of some deep values. Following the Romantic philosophers, Berlin argued that every culture possesses its own "center of gravity"—a deep value system—and we should not look to pave over these differences with imperialistic notions of universal good.[23] Instead, Berlin called for "value pluralism"—acceptance that there are many deep cultural values that are all equally correct, but that some are incompatible with each other.

My own view of favoritism and fairness is influenced by Berlin's approach. The loyalty of favoritism bumps straight into the disinterested impartiality of fairness, and you have to choose between them. You cannot have your cake and eat it too. I can choose radical egalitarianism and try to live like Gandhi, or I can choose radical favoritism and try to live like Tony Soprano. But I can't do both at the same time.

Since I have been suggesting that neither of these value choices is *intrinsically* superior, the natural questions are these: Are these differing values merely relative? Are we left with an arbitrary *relativism* of tribalism versus egalitarianism? I don't think so.

Just because we cannot find an eternal measure of justice that finally resolves the disagreement between favoritism and fairness does not mean that we are powerless to judge between them. The solution is context. The ethical life is not the bureaucratic application of fixed

Fig. 21. Sir Isaiah Berlin (1909–1997), the political philosopher who argued for "value pluralism." Berlin exercised a cosmopolitan toleration and appreciation for different value systems, but also pointed out the inevitable clash of some of these. Drawing by Stephen Asma.

rules to real-life dilemmas, nor is it a mystical intuition of transcendental Truths. By analogy: Where is a song, before it is first sung? Berlin asks this question and replies: "Nowhere is the answer—one creates the song by singing it, by composing it. So, too, life is created by those who live it, step by step. This is an aesthetic interpretation of morality and of life, not an application of eternal models. Creation is all."[24]

But we are not composing the ethical life in some unconstrained self-serving manner—a charge often leveled by the bureaucratic moralists. Rather, we can make reasonable judgments at the personal and political level by combining historical and cultural understanding with basic objective facts about human biology.[25] Combining historical, cultural, and biological knowledge informs our deep conviction that concentration camps are bad. Full stop. But other ethical disagreements are less clear. For these, we will have to take it "step by step."

"*Mozhe shitou guo he*" is a Chinese idiom that Deng Xiaoping used to describe how China should move forward.[26] Without any obvious road map, historical precedent, or abstract idealism, China was to move into the future slowly and carefully—like when you ford a river by feeling each of the stones with your feet (*Mozhe shitou guo he*).

This, I believe, is the same careful empirical approach that we should use when tribal values and egalitarian values clash—both in ourselves and in the geopolitical sphere. It is not enough, by a long shot, to say: I am of the liberal tradition, and therefore I am always against tribalism, nepotism, bias, and favoritism. I have tried to show, in this book, that there is some greater rapprochement between liberalism and tribalism, but of course there is also a limit.[27] Conflict between tribes is inevitable (as is conflict between tribalism and egalitarianism), but cooperation/consensus is not impossible.

We make these tough contextual decisions all the time, but we don't always acknowledge their improvisational nature. For example, as a teacher I have a grid of assignment grades and attendance for my students. At the end of the semester, I, like most teachers, tabulate the scores and give the grade. If the final grade was just the sum of the grid calculations, I could give the tally sheet to my third-grade son, a neighbor, or a stranger on the street and still be confident that their simple addition will produce the just grades. But I don't do it that way. In many large class institutions (e.g., 200-seat lecture halls), this sad mechanical approach is the inevitable method. But if you actually know your students, then you also know that there are many contextual aspects that cannot be put on a grading grid. This student, for example, was exemplary in their written work, but browbeat other students and lorded a sense of arrogant superiority over them. I don't have a grid category for that. This student struggled admirably in the course, but lost her mother to cancer in week six and of course never regained full momentum. I don't have a grid category for that. This student didn't test well but seemed to read every supplemental book I offhandedly mentioned in class. This student is a homophobic jerk but reads and writes with great conceptual precision. This student does B work, but texts incessantly on his cell phone while we are having class discussions. This student is not doing well at all, but I accidentally saw him playing the most transcendent Bach piano concerto in the student center. I don't have grading grid categories for any of this stuff. But I acknowledge, unapologetically, that they all play into my contextually bound judgments about students' final grades. The more experienced I get (read "older"), the *wiser* these qualitative judgments seem to get. This grading example may seem trivial, but I offer it as an example of our everyday process of "feeling the stones with our feet." Supreme, Superior, and District Court judges, presiding over complex legal cases, make similar types of judgments using sentencing guidelines, legal precedents, and other procedural strategies. If they can cultivate sensitivity to the particulars and the contexts of their cases, wisdom will prevail as they go beyond the mere application of legal rules. As Barry Schwartz and Ken Sharpe argue in *Practical Wisdom*, judges must not fall victim to the modern jeopardy of mathematical or computational justice. In recent years, mandatory sentencing rules became inflexible grids that judges dogmatically applied, but their goal of fairness was undermined by an unwillingness to factor in the subtle contextual differences in the cases. Wise judges know when and where to bend rules and improvise, in the service of justice (not in the service of self).[28]

If schlubs like me are doing this kind of wise improvising with values, and court judges are doing it, then we must accept the fact that presidents, premiers, and prime ministers are also feeling the stones with their feet. Favoritists like me wish there was more of this, not less.

But even with the most dexterous improvisers, it may be impossible to reconcile some of the dissonance between values and tribes. The British writer Evelyn Waugh noticed that the happiness and virtue of human beings is not much influenced by their larger political and economic conditions. Sinners and saints, for example, arise and thrive in every sort of political economy. Still, this did not render him neutral and disinterested in the larger tribal conflicts. "I do not think," Waugh stated, "that British prosperity is inimical to anyone else, but if, on occasion, it is, I want Britain to prosper and not her rival."[29]

On some things, you will simply have to choose between *what is loved* and *what is fair*. And on some things, you will find compatibility. But while there is no algorithm or calculus or universal grid of fairness, there is the humbler, groping method of *mozhe shitou guo he*.

7

Because You're Mine, I Walk the Line

Johnny Cash wrote that famous song about his first wife in 1956, when he was touring on the road and struggling to stay faithful. The song "I Walk the Line" is about the sacrifices and the devotions of love—the profound lengths to which we will go for our favorites. The bonds of favoritism create moral gravity and contour the way we treat people inside and outside the gravitational field. I don't walk the line for just anybody. Johnny Cash refers to the "tie that binds" and celebrates his own willingness to be constrained by the heart. This is not the realm of fairness, equality, or impartiality. But it is a moral realm of value and action, all the same.

The fact that Cash couldn't make this noble fidelity last is slightly amusing, but tolerable, I suppose, when viewed from a mature perspective on romance. He famously took a new favorite, June Carter, and the rest is history as they say. But it also reveals the obvious human *flexibility* of the "tie that binds." Some of our privileged favorites are automatically *given* (e.g., mothers, fathers, children, siblings, ethnic tribes), and some of them are freely *chosen* (e.g., spouses, friends, aesthetic and political tribes).[1]

The relationship between freedom and favoritism is complicated. On the one hand, freely choosing one's spouse is a license not afforded in many parts of the developing world. But more provocative is the possibility that it's not much of a free choice in the developed world either. Who you end up "falling for" seems (sometimes tragically) way out of your control.[2]

Freely and consciously choosing my tribe of friends or favorites offers additional pleasures on top of the other attractions involved. Every rebellious teenager knows the joys of finally choosing friends that not only supplant parental choices but actually frustrate and torture parent expectations. But rebellion or even "free choice" is much too flimsy to sustain real favoritism for very long, and the lasting bonds of attachment need sturdier validation.

The Anglo-American poet W. H. Auden claimed that American ideology reverses the traditional European value system—for Europe, virtue precedes freedom, but for Americans freedom precedes virtue. Auden noticed that America is so fiercely devoted to liberty that we would rather freely choose *vice* than have virtue forced upon us.[3] Our national stance— "You're not the boss of me"—leads us to think of freedom as an end in itself rather than a *means* to some virtuous end. This may be one of the reasons why Americans tend to think of morality as a set of rules rather than as virtues or modes of character. American values assert *freedom from* harassment and *freedom to* fulfill basic human capabilities, but positive and substantial notions of good are noticeably absent beyond this rudimentary ethical conversation. I have been suggesting that many of the substantial ingredients of the good life (i.e., bonds of family, friends, and tribe) clash incurably with our official culture of fairness. In this last part of the book, I want to remind people about the virtues of favoritism. And also offer some reflections about the *future* of favoritism, especially in the digital age.

The Virtues of Favoritism

I have not argued against obviously good egalitarian ideals, like legal due process. And I believe that ideals of fairness will have to remain dominant in the legal domain of modern nation-states. Moreover, economic and health-care disparity should be improved, and my favoritist position should not be taken as an endorsement of lassez-faire doctrine. It was not my goal to denounce *all* forms of egalitarian fairness, but to dethrone it as the standard of Western ethical life. One can see, given the large social-justice issues, why many philosophers try to draw a line that separates public and private ethics—suggesting two worlds of ethical norms. But as I've argued throughout this book, the cure for corruption and obscene wealth is not legalistic fairness, but something deeper—something in the cultivation of our common humanity. Overcoming greed and increasing charity are not just *possible* after the ideology of fairness, but we see such virtue already confirmed in non-egalitarian cultures and eras. I'm not overly Romantic about virtue-based cultures—they have room for improvement too—but many Westerners naively continue to confuse ethics with fairness.

In today's political climate, both liberals and conservatives struggle to articulate a notion of the good that accommodates individualism, tribalism, and strangers. But the Left, especially, has fallen prey to the myth of egalitarianism. The Left writhes under the neurotic push-pull of its own human attachments to family and tribe, and its contrary dogma-driven guilt about partiality and bias. Furthermore, the Left has taken a morally righteous tone in recent years by disingenuously redefining "fairness" in purely progressive terms (e.g., redistribution of wealth, affirmative action, etc.), suggesting that alternative views of justice and value (e.g., our natural nepotism) are simply forms of bigotry. As political rhetoric, this pretended piety seems advantageous, but liberals should be careful not to premise their sense of justice on a complete denial of bias—since biology usually triumphs over ideology.

The Left erroneously assumes that the "open society" cannot be achieved if favoritism is allowed to persist. Its historical response to favoritism was to level the social world on the model of universal scientific laws (see my discussion of "the grid" in chapter 3) and forbid partiality as immoral and uncivilized. I have been suggesting that liberalism confused the excesses and abuses of centralized regime kleptocracy with the more benign and meaningful forms of kin loyalty. This is understandable since liberalism was born in large part by kicking its way out of empires and monarchies. But it's time to reclaim the lost virtues of preference. What is needed is a liberalism that can admit and acknowledge our nepotistic attachments.[4]

My own trifling attempt to poeticize our culture has been to return our preferential emotional life to the center of ethics. One of the most obvious justifications for favoritism—hinted at but not yet explicitly discussed—is that it substantially increases human happiness.

In the last decade, positive psychology and neuroscience have pursued extensive research into human happiness.[5] Traditional psychology focused primarily on pathology, but positive happiness has been subjected to empirical analysis of late, and the findings are relevant for my argument. The main ingredient in human happiness is not wealth, property, pleasure, or fame, but strong social bonds. Strong friendships and family bonds are unparalleled in providing people with happiness. That doesn't mean they always give pleasure, because sometimes they are highly stressful. But pleasure is not the same as happiness, and on balance people self-report that their tribes are worth the trouble.

Many Americans are duped by flashy consumer culture into the belief that happiness comes from material wealth and limitless free choices. Subsequently, we tend to go in the wrong direction, trying to satisfy our endless desires, when we should be looking elsewhere for happiness.

My son's mother, Wen, who grew up in Mainland China, always chuckles at the American obsession with *choice*. Americans, she thinks, are quick to let go of things and people as soon as pleasure dissipates. And my Cambodian friend Naht—who spends half the year in the States and half in a village near Siem Reap, Cambodia—confirms this assessment of American whimsy. "Americans," she says, "have too many choices to be happy." Both Wen and Naht agree that too many choices lead to increased anxiety and misery, and they claim that the more obliged lifestyle, where family duty constrains your choices, actually lets you focus better and live more deeply in your activities. In America we spend a lot of time and energy trying to maximize the most satisfactory choice. We gather data about our choices and stress out about our imminent decisions. We regret many of our decisions because possibilities are so endless. We waste hours researching the best toaster oven on Amazon, or the ultimate juicer, or the most nutritious cat food. I stood frozen and motionless recently in front of a bartender who had handed me a drink menu of over two hundred microbrew beers. Frequently, all these choices leave people paralyzed and unable to commit. When they do commit, they obsess and fret over the missed opportunities that their actual choice forced upon them.

Most of us assume that more choice always means more happiness. But a recent study by psychologist Barry Schwartz suggests that Naht and Wen are correct.[6] According to recent figures published in the *Journal of the American Medical Association*, Americans are more depressed than ever. And Dr. Schwartz claims that it is because Americans, despite their relative wealth and their myriad life choices, are fundamentally *lonely*. The most important factor in happiness is close social relations, something that most Americans lack. Being connected to others, he argues, is the missing ingredient that Americans have lost in their pursuit of individual success. Materialism, prosperity, and consumer culture help to sever the traditional "ties that bind"—we're not as economically reliant on our families as those in the developing world. And then we use these same things—materialism, prosperity, and consumption—to try to fill the emotional hole. Things like demanding family obligations, serious long-lasting friendships, religious fellowship, and community closeness all bind us, but paradoxically create happier people. Throughout most of human history, these bonds were inherited, not chosen.

Americans complain of a lack of intimacy in their lives. Dr. Schwartz points out: "We spend less time visiting with neighbors. We spend less time visiting with our parents, and much less time visiting with other relatives. Partly this is because we *have* less time, since we are busy trying to determine what choices to make in other areas of life. But partly this is because close social relations have themselves become matters of choice." In other words, we used to live in a world (more like the tribal developing world) where the social bonds were simply a "given," but now we must actively cultivate fundamentals like family and friends. For example, in Cambodia your family always lives in very close proximity, usually multiple generations under the same roof. But in the States, the family can be spread out over the whole country, forcing people to work hard (and fail) at endeavors that used to be no-brainer natural conditions. Friendships also grow flimsy at continental distances, and Schwartz concludes that "our social fabric is no longer a birthright but has become a series of deliberate and demanding choices."[7]

I conclude from all of this that favoritism leads to more happiness than fairness. Happiness has been largely misunderstood as a passive state of pleasure, when it's really more like a skill—something that needs active cultivation. That is why I've discussed it here in a section on the *virtues*, where it may seem surprising. But let us now turn to some more recognizable virtues of favoritism: loyalty, generosity, and gratitude.

Loyalty

The American educator and psychologist Rensis Likert (1903–1981) argued that the real cause of group success was not top-down management but intergroup loyalty. "The greater the loyalty of a group toward the group, the greater is the motivation among the members to achieve the goals of the group, and the greater the probability that the group will achieve its goals."[8] This appears to be a general management application of an already well-known truth about successful families and tribes. If we have each other's backs, then we survive and thrive. But the thing about loyalty is that it's not premised on *optimal* conditions. You need to have my back, for example, even when I'm sometimes wrong. You need to have my back, even when I sometimes screw up the job. And I have to extend to you the same loyalty.[9]

Having a shared cause (even an arbitrary one) is a monumental aspect of the meaningful life. For one thing, it sifts out many of our

Fig. 22. The Trojan hero Aeneas (son of Aphrodite) is the Western icon of filial devotion.
When Troy was sacked by the Greeks, Aeneas (who had killed twenty-eight Greeks
in battle) narrowly escaped, but not before he saved his father and his son.
Here he is depicted carrying his elderly father and dragging his son out of harm's way.

competing desires and focuses our motivations. Loyalty also sparks a
related virtue—resoluteness. We resolve to stay the course, even when
storms try to divert us. And shared cause is what "takes over" after
the biology of family bonding does its first-tribe work, and we find
ourselves out in the free realm of competing allegiances. The average
child finds herself already allied with a given community, but as she
matures she consciously gives loyalty to new shared causes—thereby
bringing herself into meaningful community with others. Equality
and fairness have little to offer in this fundamentally biased arena of
meaning.

Loyalty and fairness seem to me to be two of the inherently clash-
ing values that Isaiah Berlin warned us about. Of course, loyalty on
its own will not be enough to set our ethical norms, and other considerations (regarding which goals we should be loyal to) will need to
inform the virtue. But in a sense, the kind of loyalty I'm praising here
is loyalty to specific people, not to "goals" or "causes." The truly loyal
person says: To hell with consequences! The egalitarian rule-follower
is merely expedient, but the loyal person will go to the wall for you.
And you're supposed to return the existential devotion.

Generosity

Another crucial virtue of favoritism is generosity. Most people ally
generosity on the side of fairness because fairness seeks to redistribute benefits and properties. But favoritists can claim selfless giving as
a virtue too. Greed is not possible in a real circle of favorites, and the
truly avaricious must separate themselves away from the bonds of family and friends in order to indulge their vice. Unlike the bureaucratic
egalitarian attempt to distribute minimal goods as far and as widely as
possible, the favoritist will lavish his loved ones with benefits that cost
blood, sweat, and tears.

As Christian egalitarianism grew and appropriated the ancient
virtues, the idea of generosity changed slightly from sharing as *philia*
(brotherly love) to sharing as *philanthropos* (love of all humanity). The
ancients had an idea of "loving all humanity," but it was embryonic
and applied more to how the gods loved the human race (e.g., Prometheus was philanthropic when he gave us fire). Generosity, in the
Christian era, became redefined as giving to the *poor* (whether we
knew the poor or not).

The virtue of generosity that may best capture the biased version is
probably *magnanimity*. This is the ancient virtue of being big-hearted
(literally, the large-souled person). This is giving without any expectation of recompense. But when we read ancients, like Aristotle and Cicero, we find that *affection* is the inner spring of this generosity. Since I
already discussed the virtue of "biased generosity" in chapter 4, I want
to turn to the correlate virtue—namely, *gratitude*.

Gratitude

It's hard for many of us to receive a gift. We do fine with birthday presents, wedding gifts, and other institutionalized generosities. But most other gifts come with strings attached, and Americans in particular are uncomfortable with the binding entanglements that strings bring. If we're raised on an ideology of self-reliance, and if our money-based economy has "freed" us from family dependence, then being grateful may not be a regular exercise for us.

In a real circle of favorites, however, one needs to accept help gracefully. We must accept, without cynicism, the fact that some of our family and friends give to us *for our own sake* (our own flourishing) and not for their eventual selfish gain. However animalistic were the evolutionary origins of giving (and however vigorous the furtive selfish genes), the human heart, neocortex, and culture have all united to eventually create true altruism. Gratitude is a necessary response in a sincere circle of favorites.

Pride is a curious thing because it puffs up whenever you know that you are someone's favorite—whether you're one of God's chosen people, or you've just been chosen first for gym-class soccer team, or the cute girl chose you at the dance. But pride can also prevent you from graciously accepting help and can fill you with resentment instead of appreciation. This is not just a psychological generalization, but a kind of existential point. It takes real effort and sensitivity to accept preferential treatment. A sense of existential worth comes along with genuine gratitude. And a rare charity toward oneself (a kind of magnanimity) must accompany the thought: *I'll gladly accept your help, and (in some cases) I'll never be able to pay you back.*[10] The idealized grid of fairness cannot limn the contours of these deep existential debts.[11]

This brings us to a brief consideration of the relationship between *character* and favoritism. One of the reasons why the grid of impartiality evolved was to prevent the privileges of class and race and gender. Stripping away the diverse content of people in order to arrive at the generic human being was good for legal jurisprudence, but problematic in other regards. People are not just biased about class, race, and gender.

In addition to the obvious biases of kith and kin that I've been focusing on, people are highly preferential toward attractive people, tall people, happy people, confident people, and charismatic people generally.

Now, here's a telling analogy. When mega-corporations like fast-food chains, for example, sought to create highly uniform branches and franchises, they fashioned extremely methodical rules for employees to adopt. If I'm the French-fry guy in a fast-food restaurant, then I am governed by a very precise set of directives that tell me what temperature to make the oil, when to add the prefabbed potatoes, when to jiggle the basket, when to pull them out, how much salt to shake, where to put the fries, how to place the heat lamps, and on and on. It's the same institutional manufacturing model that industrialization created and that Karl Marx complained about.[12] Now, worries about alienated labor aside, the thing to notice here is that *personality* has been systematically removed from institutionalized labor. Personality—with its unpredictable differences and unique mannerism, perspectives, and behaviors—is the last thing employers want on the fast-food assembly line. The more personality and charisma you add to the fry guy, the less uniform and reliable the product. The quirks of human personality are impediments to the efficiency of the system. In this regard, modern labor has sought the idealization model of physics, which often ascribes universal laws to bodies that have been mentally stripped of their respective variables and treated "as if" they were frictionless, or perfectly spherical, or perfectly elastic, or whatever.

The digital age has only strengthened this trajectory, because we increasingly think of knowledge as *information*. But information can be separated from its original medium and re-instantiated in a new one, plus an informational byte can be digitally reproduced ad nauseam. I can have some information fact come to me in an e-mail, and it can be sent to my phone, my digital work pad, my social network, my office computer—I can have it printed, change its font, project it, turn it into an audio message, and so on. The medium doesn't matter.

The grid of impartial fairness tries to do the same thing with people and ethics. Egalitarian fairness tries to separate abstract rules of right and wrong from the person. It tries to reduce our messy ethical lives to regimented fast-food-like procedures. Utilitarian, Kantian, and Rawlsian approaches to ethics make this same fatal mistake. But in the social domain—the real world of diverse people—the medium does matter. Who I am (and where I stand to kith and kin) makes all the difference.

Compare the cog-in-the machine version of the French-fry guy with the mentor-apprentice model, and you will see a better way of thinking about virtue and character. Of course, the French-fry guy doesn't need a mentor for his job—that's the "triumph" of regimented labor. But human beings do need ethical mentors.[13] The mentor-apprentice relation is one of those preferential, favoritist relations that I mentioned earlier, and it flickers still in some forms of labor and education. In modern egalitarian education, we separate out the information from the character. Uniform workbooks and lesson plans allow for almost any teacher and any student to process similar informational content. Substitute teachers can look at standardized lesson plans and pick up where the last teacher left off. But mentoring is different. As philosopher Vigen Guroian puts it, "In mentoring there is no distinction between method and content. By means of physical gesture, tone of voice, and behavior, the mentor communicates his special knowledge and skill and also a piece of his own character."[14] This intimate learning is how ethics really works. And you can't get kinder, more compassionate, and more generous people by teaching them formulas of fairness.

The intimacy of favoritism brings personal character back to the forefront of ethics, where it belongs. You don't inspire a kid to be generous or courageous by giving him a rulebook of universal moral maxims. Instead, parents or caretakers must *demonstrate* generosity and other virtues. Tribes transmit their ethics to the young by their actions, which cannot be abstracted as information. And art, too— whether it's the entertainment of Pixar and Disney movies or the biblical stories of heroism and folly—must show the virtues as concrete expressions of character. You can take the personality and charisma out of French-fry making, but not out of ethics.

You Can't Love Humanity. You Can Only Love People.

Throughout this book, I have been suggesting that fairness unfairly dominates our culture and crowds out the virtues of favoritism. Many people will disagree with this characterization, but some will actually agree and *still* resist my call for more favoritism. They argue that we need fairness (and a lot of it) to *counterbalance* the tribalism of favoritism.

The excellent social theorist Barry Schwartz has challenged my view, with what I'll call the "counterweight argument." He asks us to consider

> the possibility that the only thing that keeps favoritism within reasonable bounds is precisely our commitment to fairness. In other words, favoritism comes "naturally," but fairness does not. Maybe it takes all of our will, rational justification, and ideological commitment to fairness to keep favoritism within bounds. Were people to subscribe to [Asma's] view, perhaps the center would not hold, and we would slowly but inexorably give in to the worst of our "us vs. them" tendencies.[15]

I take this objection very seriously. My job in the book has been to promote the underdog idea that favoritism also has an ethical structure (i.e., it's not just self-interest and corruption), but maybe I've overplayed my hand to compensate. The heuristic idealism of fairness may be just the thing that constrains too much nepotism. I'm sure there's some truth in this. On the other hand, I've spent a lot of time showing that we don't really know what we're talking about when we confidently intone fairness. We frequently use "fairness" when we mean other things (e.g., tolerance, generosity, etc.), and we criticize favoritism when we mean to criticize other things. And I think it's important to raise this point again, in light of the counterweight argument.

For example, Dr. Schwartz voices a popular view, rightly suggesting that we need a counterweight to our natural preferences and biases of kin and kith, but what he means (I think) is that we need ideological reminders to motivate us to help strangers. We need a "Good Samaritan" trigger that pulls us out of our default nepotism. I agree with this, to some extent. But why are we so quick to call this fairness? And why would we need a concept like equality to motivate our Good Samaritan behaviors? Reaching out to strangers actually looks more like charity and compassion, which often get confusedly labeled as "fairness" but shouldn't be.

If you plug in the word and—more importantly—the act of *charity* (where we ordinarily use "fairness"), we find that the sought-after moral upgrade is still achieved: the less fortunate become better off than before. People who are triggered to charitable acts share their good fortune with others. But it isn't fairness that accomplishes this moral goal—it isn't the pursuit of equality; it is kindness, goodwill, and dare I say a little bit of "favor" (in this case, for strangers).

In our current culture, the language of fairness is ubiquitous around this kind of charitable benevolence toward strangers, but it shouldn't be. Sadly, there is not enough of this compassion in our contemporary culture, but it doesn't improve matters to incorrectly call it fairness and expect egalitarian rules or calculations to fix it. Our charity to strangers is not motivated by the idea that they are our equals, or that they have equal claim on us as our kith and kin have, or that they merit our goodwill by some excellent achievements, or that they have human rights, or that we're restoring some imbalance in the social system. When we move beyond the civil courtesy that we owe to strangers and we donate to some cause or give to someone on the street or whatever, it is because we're moved by sympathy. We are stirred to care about these particular sufferers. We identify with them emotionally. Love, not fairness, is the engine of philanthropy, and the counterbalance of too much kin favoritism is a more broadly cast affection. But, of course, there's a limit to the breadth of one's affection, for as Graham Greene reminds us: "One can't love humanity, one can only love people."[16]

As I write this, the Occupy Wall Street movement is in full swing. I don't know where it will be in a year from now, but it is currently an exciting time. People from all sides of the political continuum are calling for radical change in America's obnoxious wealth gap—wherein the top 20 percent of Americans own 85 percent of the country's wealth, and the bottom 80 percent own a mere 15 percent of the wealth.

The counterweight arguers, like Barry Schwartz, might use the Occupy Wall Street movement as a strong objection to my call for favoritism. See what favoritism, unchecked by fairness, gets you? The Occupy movement, one might argue, is trying to reset the scale toward greater fairness. After all, the movement regularly intones the language of fairness, and journalist Charlie Rose referred to the movement as "all about fairness." But while I like and support the movement generally, I don't think it should be characterized as an egalitarian crusade of fairness.

Closer examination of the movement does not reveal a call for equality of wealth or goods. It is not a communist quest for redistribution of wealth along egalitarian lines. The protestors want the wealthy to pay their respective taxes, not have their property seized and redistributed to the proletariat. Moreover, the protestors are disgusted by federal bank bailouts and corporate protections, while middle-class housing collapses, jobs disappear, and wage and benefits protections vanish. It is also the injustice of the disproportionate distribution of debt burden that inflames the movement. The Occupy movement is a cry for justice, but not a cry for fairness.

Underneath the varied and sometimes incoherent demands of the Occupy movement is an objection to the entire culture of profit and consumption. The cracked economy has forced reflection on the younger generation—who are entering the job market for the first time without the prospect of expanding innovative bubbles (like manufacturing, dot-coms, housing, etc.). Graduating with massive debt and facing "careers" like coffee barista and waiter have not only created despair about joining the upwardly mobile American dream, but have also created questions about the dream itself—consumerism and capitalism.

The deeper discontent under the Occupy movement is not unfairness, but a lack of community, creativity, and meaning in a society that currently defines all these successes in materialistic terms. Corruption and abuse of power are high on the list of complaints, but people also want more stability and security (e.g., housing and job security), more community, decent health care, less debt (e.g., staggering education loans), less stress, and less alienation from the meaningful aspects of life (e.g., the rat race makes family and even friendships more fractured). Most of these complex grievances about social justice get reduced down to cries for greater "fairness" because we lack a more nuanced moral vocabulary. But most Occupiers are not calling on political leaders and the wealthy to treat them as entitled to equal shares of wealth or even equal opportunities. They want the privileged class and the corrupt policy makers to open their eyes to the suffering of the underprivileged, and to stop policies that increase that suffering—and, positively, to create policies that ameliorate such suffering and even contribute to the happiness of the majority. It's hard to see how ideas of fairness help here, except in the trivial sense that hard work should reap more deserts than the current system apportions (i.e., the merit-based notion of fairness).

The counterweight argument—that fairness checks excessive favoritism—accepts the idea that fairness may be unrealistic, overly idealistic, and even wrong, but if we remove this egalitarian tradition, we will be in worse shape. I appreciate this warning—that I should be careful what I wish for. On the other hand, we have the much older virtue tradition of giving, generosity, magnanimity, and compassion, which has atrophied during the rise of instrumental modernity but which can ably inspire the needed Good Samaritan values.

I'm not suggesting a conservative return to religious values here. Instead, I am isolating the emotional engine of motivation that lives underneath both secular and sacred forms of charity. Nepotistic virtues like loyalty are emotion driven, but Good Samaritan virtue toward strangers is also emotionally driven. It is the affective connection or concern—which thrives in tribalism, but also stimulates philanthropy beyond immediate circles.

Cosmopolitan thinkers voice a version of the counterweight argument when they call us to adopt a different set of *public* values than the more biased domain of *private* values. From Immanuel Kant's autonomous agent to contemporary notions of a public "thin self," the liberal cosmopolitan view has decontextualized people in order to protect against bias and favoritism.

My view, however, is hard to square with the cosmopolitan views of universal decontextualized agents. Like the communitarian philosophers (e.g., Michael Walzer, Charles Taylor, Alasdair MacIntyre, and Michael Sandel), I reject the disembodied approach of egalitarianism, but I'm offering something new here too. The communitarians all stress the community of "tradition" in opposition to egalitarianism. They think community comes from being Catholic or Jewish or French Canadian or some other linguistic, ritualistic, or ideological tribe. But my view is that true communities are "affective communities"—emotional bonds precede cultural/historical/linguistic traditions, though they certainly feed into one another. This unappreciated point reveals the true bond underlying cultural tradition and also highlights the flexibility and changeable nature of favoritism and tribalism. If being Catholic or Jewish failed to give us affective community, then we would undoubtedly keep searching. Being Catholic or Jewish, for example, is not an end in itself, but a means to an emotional end.

The Future of Favoritism

Technology is a double-edged sword. It clears the obstructions ahead, but also severs the ties that bind. Sigmund Freud, in his *Civilization and Its Discontents*, weighs the positive and the negative. Modern technological culture, he says, can bring me my faraway son's voice on the telephone or provide me with a cable that notifies me of my friend's safe arrival in a distant country. But, taking up the opposite side, he points out, "If there had been no railway to conquer distances, my child would never have left his native town and I should need no telephone to hear his voice; if traveling across the ocean by ship had not been introduced, my friend would not have embarked on his sea-voyage and I should not need a cable to relieve my anxiety about him."[17] These examples sound quaint to us now, of course, but the recent technological jumps have only strengthened this debate, not put it to rest.

We live in the digital age of high-speed Internet connections, Twitter, Facebook, avatar egos, and apps for everything. All around the developed world, some kids are so addicted to computer gaming that parents and community leaders have created intervention services to detox them. People can spend increasingly larger chunks of their lives in the simulacrum—working, playing, and socializing. What does all this mean for deep tribal connections?

As I write this, Google is just rolling out its own social network system, called the Google+ project. And one of the fascinating features is something called "Circles," which allow you to encircle your friends and family into tight groups of favorites—making privileged or intimate communication faster and more cohesive. In the promotional video, a man describes how hesitant he is to take on new friends, because he recognizes the energy that real friendship requires. He shares his musings with us, asking himself: "Will this new person, trying to enter my circle of favorites, be worth it?" And in the end, he decides to take a chance on the new contender for circle status. Google seems to hold out the promise that we'll be so popular in digital land, that we'll need to carefully weigh people's incoming supplications.

One of my younger friends excitedly told me that he was up to a thousand "friends" on Facebook. When I said, "You can't have a thousand friends," he took me to be questioning his veracity. But I clarified. You, or anyone else, cannot have a thousand friends because friendship is not the kind of thing that can be spread so widely. He seemed to think that since two friends are better than one, and three are better than two, then a thousand is even better. If this is where we're heading, then we're in trouble.

The profound need for social interaction is so nakedly clear in the new media world, that it sometimes borders on heartbreaking. Microsoft rolled out its new social media–sharing phone, targeted for Generation Y users, calling it simply "Kin." And it promises in ads to "help you manage your social life." Of course, the idea that your social world is "manageable" (or that it *should* be manageable) is extremely questionable. Managing your tribe is like managing the weather.

Our lack of meaningful tribal bonds might also play a role in the recent profusion of genealogical websites, which allow users to search and build family trees. It seems that we need more deep human contact in our lives, but it also seems dubious that the virtual world of managed "favorite circles" and "eager contenders" can ever deliver on its prosthetic promise of community.

We might talk about "tribes" loosely as the group of people in our digital social network that "like" the same music and news stories, and who write witty quips next to one another's posts, but that is only a tribe in the most shallow sense. On social networking sites, one finds all kinds of idiosyncratic groups, like "Stepmothers who like chocolate milkshakes at 1 am while watching reruns of *Oprah*."[18] But a real tribe doesn't just click approvingly on your tweets and photos. They bring you soup when you're sick; they watch your kids in an emergency; they open professional doors for you; they rearrange their schedules for you; they protect you; they fight for you; they *favor* you—and you return all this hard work. Because your care, time, and energy are *finite*, you can only have a small tribe of favorites. The brain's affective/emotional system, a limited resource, must glue tribes together. The digital world adds *breadth* but not *depth* to human connections (the exception is when you already have some depth with a friend in the real world and can enhance it in the digital realm).

The growing model of social interaction as controllable, comfortable, and convenient is disturbing because it suggests that relationships can be made-to-order. The computer software designer David Levy proposes, in his book *Love and Sex with Robots*, that in the near future many people will overcome their social anxieties by entering into intimate relations with robots.[19] Levy is cheerful about the idea that outcasts will not have to get their hearts broken, their hopes dashed, their schedules inconvenienced by flesh-and-blood intimates. Technology will solve the discomforts of social life.

I'm not a Luddite, and I can't wait for robots to clean my house, but I take umbrage at the notion that the discomforts of social life should be "fixed" with technology. We may eventually find the "always on" digital generation to be a group of wilting flowers, if they have sidestepped every uncomfortable tribal demand by technological means. It's reminiscent of people who don't have enough fortitude to be in a real tribe, so they surround themselves with cats and other pliable pets instead.

Being in a tribe is hard. There's no way around that. It might even turn out that the *struggle* between intimates is as much a part of the affective bonding as the pleasure. But one thing is clear. If you want people to go to the wall for you (and I don't mean your Facebook wall), then get off your computer and *do* something with them—preferably something high stakes, something you would only do for a favorite, something beyond what they "fairly" deserve.

The Archbishop and the Chambermaid

The impulse to equality and fairness is thought to be our highest principle, but in many specific contexts it short-circuits, loses coherence, and even violates some of our deeper values. I've tried to rescue

Fig. 23. William Godwin's famous Archbishop versus Chambermaid thought experiment. I know who I'm saving. Drawing by Stephen Asma.

nepotism from corruption, affirm justice in the absence of fairness, and praise tribal devotion in a world of strangers.

My hope is that other thinkers will follow my lead and try to find ways to integrate preferentialism into Western liberalism, but also adopt enough realism to acknowledge the unfixable value clashes when they arise. Tribal values certainly dominated before the rise of liberalism, and now liberalism (as the grid of impartiality) has certainly had a few centuries in the sun. It's time, I submit, for a new injection of some old-school favoritism.

One of the architects of modern utilitarian ethics was William Godwin (1756–1836), a philosopher who formulated a famous thought experiment and is an intellectual progenitor of contemporary ethicists like Peter Singer. He asked us to imagine if you could only save one person from a burning building. One of those persons is Archbishop Fénelon and the other is a common chambermaid. Furthermore, the archbishop is just about to compose his famous work *The Adventures of Telemachus* (an influential defense of human rights). Now, here's the rub. The chambermaid is your mother.

Godwin argues that the utilitarian principle (i.e., the greatest good for the greatest number) requires you to save the archbishop rather than your mother. He asks, "What magic is there in the pronoun 'my,' that should justify us in overturning the decisions of impartial truth?"[20]

What magic? No magic, I submit. But everything else of value lies contained in that little word "my."

NOTES

Chapter One

1. See Martha Nussbaum, *From Disgust to Humanity* (Oxford University Press, 2010), 32.

2. See the conclusion section of Darwin, *Descent of Man* (Penguin Classics, 2004), 680.

3. See Bertrand Russell, "Has Religion Made Useful Contributions to Civilization?" in *Why I Am Not a Christian* (Simon and Schuster, 1957), 34.

4. Originally published in the *Partisan Review* in January 1949, George Orwell's "Reflections on Gandhi" appears in *The Orwell Reader* (Mariner Books, 1961), 331.

5. Ibid., 331.

6. See Joseph Lelyveld's discussion of their friendship in *Great Soul: Mahatma Gandhi and His Struggle with India* (Knopf, 2011).

7. A more infamous tradition, social Darwinism, followed Darwin's revolution and argued that societies should struggle for existence and engage in a survival of the fittest contest. Some economists, imperialists, and members of the leisured classes claimed that humans should indulge their natural selfishness. This lamentable tradition has a terrible track record, and one can be thankful that it is now moribund. But those who were closest to Charles Darwin, like Thomas Huxley, argued that human morality should never be modeled on the natural selection mechanism. See Huxley's 1893 essay "Evolution and Ethics." Darwin himself claimed that affection was part of the instinc-

tual equipment possessed by all social animals, so selfish individualism was *not* the inevitable default position of going native.

8. The assumption was very strong during the heyday of social Darwinism, but of course it goes back to the philosopher Thomas Hobbes (1588–1679) and even appears (very articulately) as far back as Glaucon's arguments in Plato's *Republic*.

9. Peter Corning's *The Fair Society* (University of Chicago Press, 2011) contains many great insights and nuanced discussions about fairness. I see many shared interests between our respective projects. But he, like most egalitarians, also fails to appreciate or even notice the positive aspects of an ethics of favoritism.

10. See Lawrence Rosen, "What Is a Tribe, and Why Does It Matter?," in *The Culture of Islam: Changing Aspects of Contemporary Muslim Life* (University of Chicago Press, 2002).

11. John Rawls, "Justice as Fairness," *Philosophical Review* 67, no. 2 (April 1958): 177.

12. In his *Inequality Reexamined* (Harvard University Press, 1992), philosopher and economist Amartya Sen points out that there is much confusion in political theorizing about "equality" and "fairness." If we shift the "space" or "domain" of inquiry (the locus) of human activity, we get very different maps of inequality. An equality of income between two parties may not match equality in other important domains: happiness, liberty, rights, opportunities, and so on. Nonetheless, while acknowledging Sen's caveat about diversity of domains, a common concern animates most liberal theorizing about egalitarianism. John Rawls, Ronald Dworkin, Thomas Nagel, and Sen himself are largely concerned with two things—equality of liberty/freedom and equality of primary goods.

13. Of course, egalitarianism is not as prevalent in the Bible as many assume. Right from the beginning, God favors Abel over Cain, for example, then comes Noah's lucky break, and the entire Old Testament can be read as Yahweh taking care of his oppressed chosen people.

14. See the chapter "Inescapable Frameworks" in Charles Taylor, *Sources of the Self* (Harvard University Press, 1990), 9.

15. Psychologist Wendy Mogel tells this story to journalist Lori Gottlieb at the Atlantic.com, as a video companion to Gottlieb's story "How to Land Your Kid in Therapy," *Atlantic*, July/August 2011.

16. See Adam Bellow's study *In Praise of Nepotism* (Doubleday, 2003). Bellow's book is a sprawling *history* of nepotism, and while it makes some compelling points, it is largely concerned with nepotism among the aristocracy. My own interest in favoritism is more *philosophical* than historical, and I will emphasize how favoritism cuts across all social classes—indeed, I will contend that it thrives more in non-aristocratic classes. See my discussion of positive nepotism in low-income immigrant groups in chapter 6.

17. See Rosen, *The Culture of Islam*, 13.

18. Rosen continues: "In this sense corruption can be seen as interfering with 'the game,' as getting in the way of the formation of negotiated ties of interdependency by which society is held together and by which individuals form the associations in terms of which they are themselves known." Ibid., 13.

19. See John Belden Scott, *Images of Nepotism: The Painted Ceilings of Palazzo Barberini* (Princeton University Press, 1991).

20. People frequently confuse favoritism per se with kleptocracy and corruption, but I will endeavor to disentangle them later in the book.

21. Kongzi, *Analects*, XIII.18.

22. Bertrand Russell, "Eastern and Western Ideals of Happiness," in *Sceptical Essays* (Routledge, 1977), 88.

23. Kongzi, *Analects*, XIV.36.

24. "Yet we must not on that account shrink from the task," Aristotle says, "but decide the question as best we can." See *Nicomachean Ethics*, trans. W. D. Ross, in *The Basic Works of Aristotle*, ed. Richard McKeon (Random House, 1941), bk. IX, chap. 2.

25. Ibid., bk. VIII, chap. 9.

26. Sigmund Freud, *Civilization and Its Discontents* (Norton, 1961), 82.

27. See Plato's Euthyphro in *Euthyphro, Apology, Crito and Phaedo*, trans. B. Jowett (Prometheus Books, 1988), 11.

28. I regularly ask my college students if they would protect their fathers in the *Euthyphro* scenario. Their responses are interesting. Oftentimes students' first responses cannot be trusted, because they're at pains to appear virtuous and often tell teachers what they think teachers want to hear. The problem of obtaining veracity is complicated by the fact that if I press them for more "honest" answers and they change their responses (which is often the case), I may well be inadvertently "leading" them again (like a lawyer leading a jury). All that aside, they usually say that they'd protect their father if the worker's death was *accidental*, but not if it was *murder*. When I ask them why they wouldn't protect in the case of murder, they usually hem and haw and then say: "Well, if it was murder, then he could do it again to someone else—even murder me!" When I ask the *why* question to the few students who claim they'd shelter the father even in the case of murder, they usually reply simply, "Because he's my dad." They don't see the need, or even the possibility, of further justification. I'm not sure whether the students' lack of further articulation is a scarcity of cleverness, or simply the result of running into a wall of devotion so fundamental that one tolerates no further chatterings of reason and rhetoric. I suspect it's the latter.

29. Cicero, *De Officiis*, 1.50.

Chapter Two

1. Robert Nozick, *Philosophical Explanations* (Harvard University Press, 1981).

2. Peter Singer, *The Expanding Circle: Ethics and Sociobiology* (Farrar, Straus and Giroux, 1981), 101. I am indebted to Christina Hoff Sommers, whose article "Filial Morality" examines Singer's thought experiment. Sommers makes a very compelling case for filial obligations as special moral relations. *Journal of Philosophy* 83, no. 8 (1986): 439–56.

3. See Peter Singer, *The Life You Can Save: Acting Now to End World Poverty* (Random House, 2009), 135. Singer recognizes that family bonds will usually trump the demands of strangers (as a descriptive fact of human behavior), but he draws the line when a parent's biases provide *luxuries* to children while strangers starve to death. This last point is one that I agree with, but it's unclear how Singer reconciles *any* family partiality with

his abiding dedication to utilitarian rationality. Preference utilitarianism tries to marry the subjectivities of individual values with the demands of "greatest good" egalitarianism, but the marriage seems more like a shotgun wedding.

4. See Frans de Waal, "Sympathy," in *Good Natured* (Harvard University Press, 1997).

5. Dr. Jaak Panksepp's work has been influential on my understanding of emotions, as well as more abstruse philosophical subjects, like the brain-based core of self-consciousness. His book *Affective Neuroscience: The Foundations of Human and Animal Emotions* (Oxford University Press, 1998) should be required reading for psychologists, philosophers, and cognitive scientists. My discussion of the CARE system is indebted to his book, his many scholarly papers (including "On the Embodied Neural Nature of Core Emotional Affects," *Journal of Consciousness Studies* 12 [2005]: 158–84), and personal conversations.

6. Jaak Panksepp uses capitalized versions of these common terms to indicate specific neurochemical pathways and processes underlying observable emotional states. Rage has an observable set of animal behaviors, but RAGE is the brain-based prerequisite process that gives rise to (or accompanies) those animal behaviors. I have preserved Panksepp's convention here because I think it's helpful in distinguishing the observed emotions from the (less observable) brain-based affective systems, all the while maintaining the causal relatedness of the two phenomena (e.g., care and CARE).

7. The same triggering of maternal behaviors in non-mother rats can be achieved by directly injecting oxytocin (OT) into their brains (OT can't cross the blood-brain barrier). Studies like these have also established that OT is necessary for the onset of maternal behaviors, but not the maintenance of mothering activities. Once OT flips the switch, mothering care is sustained on its own momentum, so to speak. See Thomas R. Insel, "The Neurobiology of Affiliation: Implications for Autism," in *Handbook of Affective Sciences*, ed. Richard J. Davidson, Klaus R. Scherer, and H. Hill Goldsmith (Oxford University Press, 2002).

8. See K. M. Kendrick, E. B. Keverne, and B. A. Baldwin, "Intracerebroventricular Oxytocin Stimulates Maternal Behaviour in the Sheep," *Neuroendocrinology* 46 (1987): 56–61. Endocrinologists Kendrick and Keverne have published extensively in this area of study over the last two decades.

9. Oxytocin probably evolved from the ancient brain molecule vasotocin, which regulates sexual activity in reptiles. The evolution of oxytocin also reminds us of the way that natural selection conserves available resources, repurposing their original adaptive functions into new functions. The neurochemistry of mothering and nurturing seems to be a reconfiguration of sex chemistry (oxytocin plays a role in orgasm), rather than some unprecedented adaptational jump in brain chemistry. See Panksepp, *Affective Neuroscience*, chap. 12.

10. Among mammals, infanticide is a very common albeit horrifying mechanism by which males enter a new territory and take over. When a male, whether it's a rat or a lion, enters new territory, it usually kills the babies of the group. This activity stops breastfeeding, which causes lactation to cease in the mothers, which in turn restarts ovulation. This brutal pattern creates the opportunity for the new male to mate with the females and create a new gene line. In rats, the post-coital oxytocin spike correlates

exactly with the gestation period (three weeks) of its own offspring. In other words, after sex, males calm down long enough to bond with their own offspring (not kill them), and then they slowly resume normal levels of pup killing.

11. Would it be ill-mannered to suggest that men might be better fathers if they had more sex?

12. Such similarities are technically referred to as "homologies" to indicate that they are the result of shared descent, and not merely accidental, coincidental, or analogical similarities. See my *Following Form and Function* (Northwestern University Press, 1996), for a history of the contentious homology issue.

13. See Alison B. Wismer Fries, T. E. Ziegler, J. R. Kurian, S. Jacoris, and S. Pollak, "Early Experience in Humans Is Associated with Changes in Neuropeptides Critical for Regulating Social Behavior," *Proceedings of the National Academy of Sciences* 102, no. 47 (November 2005): 17237–40.

14. Dualists of the Cartesian variety (still quite active in philosophy of mind circles) will balk at the idea that chemical process and emotional feeling are the same. Dualists recognize the *correlation* of brain process and mental experience but demand some autonomy for mental life and generally see my sort of analysis (of the chemistry of bonding) as too reductionistic. From this vantage point, the dualist also feels justified in maintaining a strict fact/value distinction and rejects the idea that brain science can tell us anything useful about ethics. But I accept Spinoza's dual-aspect monism as a more fruitful way to think about the brain-mind. Monists like myself (and most affective neuroscientists) think of subjective feelings (like care or rage) as identical with the chemical brain changes. Feelings and chemical processes are different sides (aspects) of the same coin, so to speak.

15. See Thomas R. Insel, "The Neurobiology of Affiliation: Implications for Autism," in *Handbook of Affective Sciences*, ed. Richard J. Davidson, Klaus R. Scherer, and H. Hill Goldsmith (Oxford University Press, 2002).

16. Homeostasis means "steady state" and is an important concept for understanding everything from the human cell to the human brain. Our brains have an ever-changing internal milieu of fluids, pressures, chemicals, and electrical activities, all shifting slightly (and sometimes radically) to adapt to external environmental changes (e.g., thermoregulation is a shifting concert of adjustments that tries to establish a comfortable operating temperature—a steady-state homeostasis—for our bodies, as we alternately encounter hot, sunny exposure, cold windy nights, and all points in between). Just as thermoregulation is a homeostatic system (or blood-glucose regulation), so are other brain-based processes. Emotional changes can be affective chemical imbalances that eventually restore back to balance or mood equilibrium (homeostasis). And some neuroscientists suggest that our feeling state of relaxed pleasure (equilibrium) is a correlate for a physiochemical state of homeostasis. See N. Campbell, J. Reece, L. Mitchell, *Biology*, 5th ed. (Benjamin/Cummings, Addison Wesley Longman, 1999), chap. 40.

17. Interestingly, oxytocin has been shown to also boost endogenous opioid production in the brain, by gating or preventing the usual "tolerance effect" of opioids. This may mean that filial chemistries of oxytocin work in tandem with opioids to increase the pleasures of nurturing and being nurtured. See Panksepp, *Affective Neuroscience*, chap. 13; and also R. A. Depue and J. V. Morrone-Strupinsky, "A Neurobehavioral

Model of Affiliative Bonding: Implications for Conceptualizing a Human Trait of Affiliation," *Behavioral and Brain Sciences* 28 (2005): 313–95.

18. Skepticism about the value of neuroscientific explanations is still abundant, and with good reason. Overly excited media and even researchers can draw simplistic generalizations from brain studies. It's worth noting that my own description of the early development of bonding might work fine with no other appeal than human behavior. Why bother digging into the hormones and the brain for corroboration of what behavior already indicates? The answer is that a purely behavioral approach would miss two important points for my overall argument. One, we now understand that many of these nurturing and bonding behaviors are directly underwritten by the biochemical changes I detail, so articulation of the biology component hinders the relativistic, "social constructionist" interpretation of bonding behavior (the still-dominant but dubious interpretation in the humanities and social sciences). More importantly, talking about behaviors primarily keeps us from appreciating one of my central claims: that having early prototype favorites (being bonded in early childhood and afterward) feels good. The mysterious "black box" of inner-felt subjectivity eluded behaviorists for decades, but neuroscience is now illuminating the inner emotional experiences. Behaviors are triggered by feelings, and pleasurable feelings of intimacy are crucial in creating the community of my favorites.

19. In addition to these more obvious cases of family bias through emotional association, we have recent data of other kinds of mental bias based on earlier sensory associations. R. B. Zajonc shows, in his "Exposure Effects: An Unmediated Phenomenon," that musical tone sequences previously encountered by a subject were almost always preferred to novel sequences—even when the subject had no conscious recollection of the earlier sequence and even when the sequence was delivered too rapidly for the subject to identify. See Zajonc's article in *Feelings and Emotions: The Amsterdam Symposium*, ed. Antony S. R. Manstead, Nico Frijda, and Agneta Fischer (Cambridge University Press, 2004), 194–203.

20. Panksepp, *Affective Neuroscience*, 256.

21. The exact quote is from George Eliot's *Adam Bede*. "What greater thing is there for two human souls, than to feel that they are joined for life . . . to be one with each other in silent unspeakable memories at the moment of the last parting?" See *Four Novels of George Eliot* (Wordsworth Editions, 2005), 361.

22. It's important to acknowledge that family bonding is not all fluffy happy sunshine or drug-like euphoria. Far from it. George Bernard Shaw once said, "When our relatives are at home, we have to think of all their good points or it would be impossible to endure them." *Heartbreak House* (Echo Library, 2006), 43. More seriously, some mammals are terrible parents. Grizzly bear fathers must be run out of the territory by their pregnant female mates just before they give birth, or the fathers will eat their own cubs. One wonders if an increase of oxytocin levels in male bears at this time would eliminate the infanticide behavior. But regardless of these anomalies, I've been describing an evolved affective system for solving some specific survival challenges (e.g., offspring, siblings, and parents locking on to one another, etc.). It's not a perfect system, because it doesn't *need* to be. And in humans it can fail (bad parenting, isolation, etc.) or be overwritten with powerful bonds of obligation/duty (that are negative and fear

based) rather than love (positive). Moreover, social interaction generally can be incredibly awkward and nothing like euphoria. But I don't take these data as counterevidence, because on balance the system, albeit flawed, is very successful at fastening together small collectives. And that's how *Homo sapiens* have survived.

23. I'm indebted to personal communication with social theorist Barry Schwartz, who helped me better articulate this controversial point. He kindly acted as intellectual midwife on this point, and I don't presume to ascribe this view to him personally.

24. It is no longer enough (nor is it testable) to ascribe early nuclear bonding to sublimated incestual drives (Oedipus and Electra complexes), as psychoanalysts have suggested.

25. The quote is from an NPR *Fresh Air* interview (March 14, 2011). For the fuller story see Frank Calabrese Jr. with Keith Zimmerman, Kent Zimmerman, and Paul Pompian, *Operation Family Secrets: How a Mobster's Son and the FBI Brought Down Chicago's Murderous Crime Family* (Broadway Books, 2011).

26. In other words, the default biology between mammal parents and offspring is CARE or bonding, but negative emotions—from abuse or perceived abuse—can be written over the default code. Neurologist Antonio Damasio has developed a mechanism, called a "somatic marker," to explain this flexible restructuring of the feeling brain. A somatic marker is the result of a brain process that codes experiences with emotional tone or coloration, engraving memories with affective associations that automatically and rapidly influence decision making. Rational deliberation is already heavily tilted or weighted in a certain direction by emotional biases. These biases result, in part, from somatic markers that have been stored in the ventromedial prefrontal cortex of the brain. Original codings can be changed or modified pursuant to new experiences. See extensive discussions of somatic markers in Damasio's *Descartes' Error* (Putnam, 1994) and *The Feeling of What Happens* (Harcourt Brace, 1999).

27. "Epigenetics" is the technical term for the growing study of this middle ground between nature (DNA) and nurture (environment). The brain is capable of significant reorganization depending on the kinds of input experiences. Epigenetic on/off switches control gene expression and seem capable of almost Lamarckian levels of inheritance. This is especially true in the early years of childhood development, but the brain also becomes more adaptable and open to reorganization after traumatic injuries.

28. See John Maynard Smith, "Group Selection and Kin Selection," *Nature* 201 (March 1964), for one of the definitive early statements on the evolution of groups. Biologist and philosopher Michael Ghiselin has also persuasively argued that species themselves should be understood as *individuals* (and targets of selection) rather than as *classes* of individual organisms. See Ghiselin, *Metaphysics and the Origin of Species* (SUNY Press, 1997). Interpreting the group as an individual or recognizing kin selection of groups are both ways of isolating the same fact: selection operates at the level of populations too.

29. Social evolution is of course a remarkably complex phenomenon, aided by many causal processes. Even kin selection is an umbrella term that covers many processes besides behavioral adaptation. For a sophisticated discussion of the uniquely human mechanisms of social evolution, see Kim Sterelny's work, in particular *Thought in a Hostile World: The Evolution of Human Cognition* (Wiley-Blackwell, 2003). His recent

suggestion of how "apprentice learning" evolved in early humans provides a compelling alternative to the modular evolutionary psychology approach. It would be interesting to see his same "information transmission" approach applied beyond his current concerns with craft skills, to the ethical education of our ancestors. One wonders how fairness and favoritism were scaffolded up from humble origins to the level of transmittable social norms.

30. Gould continues, "For example, in most sexually reproducing organisms, an individual shares (on average) one-half the genes of his sibs and one-eighth the genes of his first cousins. Hence, if faced with a choice of saving oneself alone or sacrificing oneself to save more than two sibs or eight first cousins, the Darwinian calculus favors altruistic sacrifice; for in so doing, an altruist actually increases his won genetic representation in future generations." Stephen Jay Gould, "Biological Potentiality vs. Biological Determinism," in *Ever Since Darwin: Reflections in Natural History* (Norton, 1979), 255.

31. An excellent discussion of group selection, especially as it helped to create the human cooperation explosion, can be found in Sterelny, *Thought in a Hostile World*, chap. 7.

32. See Jerry O'Wolff and Paul Sherman, *Rodent Societies: An Ecological and Evolutionary Perspective* (University of Chicago Press, 2007). Also see John Hoogland, *The Black-Tailed Prairie Dog: Social Life of a Burrowing Animal* (University of Chicago Press, 1995).

33. In the spring of 2011, a hot debate emerged in the pages of *Nature* surrounding a recent about-face by Edward O. Wilson, one of the earliest and best popularizers of kin selection. Wilson has changed his mind about the power of kin selection to explain altruism. He now favors a distinct causal mechanism called "group selection" (sometimes confused with kin selection) that operates in social creatures who are not necessarily related. In other words, he reverses the order of selection. Creatures that live in collectives evolved cooperative behaviors first (based only on group membership) and later this cooperation intensified for genetically related kin groups. The majority of the scientific community has roundly rejected Wilson's new suggestion, but it is still a live issue. For Wilson's controversial paper, see Martin A. Nowak, Corina E. Tarnita, and Edward O. Wilson, "The Evolution of Eusociality," *Nature* 466 (August 26, 2010): 1057–62. For scathing critiques, see *Nature* 471 (March 24, 2011): E5–E6, online.

34. Many evolutionary psychologists have argued unconvincingly, I think, for hardwired behavioral *modules* that solve these survival problems. According to thinkers like Steven Pinker, Leda Cosmides, John Tooby, and Marc Hauser, specific altruistic behaviors in animals (e.g., self-sacrifice) or cognitive skills in humans (e.g., cheater-detection skills) are brain circuits that mechanically (or computationally) solve the relevant challenge. This approach fits well with both the computational model of mind from cognitive science and the behaviorism model from animal science, but I think it's wrong. Instead, I think that affective systems (e.g., CARE, RAGE, SEEKING, etc.) are originally engraved in the brain and body of animals, and then epigenetic development and environment conditioning "educate" those feelings into complex behavioral tendencies. In other words, *inner feelings* (always treated skeptically by behaviorists) guide the preferential behaviors of altruistic animals. The chirping squirrel *feels* more panic when

its own family is in danger, and so increases its alert calls. We still need more empirical work to validate this complex model (and one should always be vigilant against unwarranted anthropomorphism), but it is more compelling than the evolutionary psychology idea that a closed computational circuit comes pre-wired in the brain.

35. What's missing in my series of extrapolating questions is something significant, but not very popular in contemporary ethical discussions. It is the *intrinsic*, dare I say spiritual, value of granting favors. The ancients would not be able to go from monkey justice to egalitarian laws without some serious consideration of the soul's or the psyche's health. The cost-benefit analysis of benevolent action was well known to them, but they argued for a more primordial reason for good deeds—namely, that they are pleasing to the soul (they are their own reward). Seneca says that he doesn't give favor to his friends because he wants favors returned "in a circle." Echoing Greeks like Plato and Aristotle, Seneca believes that virtuous giving is its own reward. He explains, "The wages of a good deed is to have done it. I am grateful, not in order that my neighbor, provoked by the earlier act of kindness, may be more ready to benefit me, but simply in order that I may perform a most pleasant and beautiful act; I feel grateful, not because it profits me, but because it pleases me." Seneca, *Ad Lucilium epistulae morales*, vol. 2 (Loeb Classical Library, Harvard University Press, 1962), epistle LXXXI, "On Benefits."

36. Matt Ridley assumes the more pessimistic social contract view of "egocentric individual first" and social cohesion later, in *The Origins of Virtue* (Penguin, 1996). He recognizes an alternative "origin story"—a communist utopia of "all for all" (instead of "all against all"). On this collectivist utopian view (still popular on the far Left), selfishness is a fall from grace, brought on by proto-capitalist inequities in the distribution of goods. Ridley lampoons this, and maybe he's right to do so. But my argument is different. The family is the small tribe at the very origin of each human's development, so it is before *both* the egotist and the altruist (it is not derivative). Family is the original tribe that acts as the nursery for hatching out the subsequent values (selfishness and selflessness).

37. See Frans de Waal's Tanner Lecture, included as part 1 in *Primates and Philosophers: How Morality Evolved* (Princeton University Press, 2009), 6–8.

38. See S. Brosnan and F. de Waal, "Monkeys Reject Unequal Pay," *Nature* 425 (2003): 297–99.

39. A contentious debate in the evolution of mind is whether animals need cognitive skills (i.e., theory of mind, or intentional stance, etc.) in order to recognize the agency of other creatures, or if these complex social hierarchies are navigated instead by precognitive skills (i.e., sensory-motor and affective patterns). This is relevant to the question of how fairness might have evolved. Does an animal have to have a theory of intentions to recognize that its tribal companion is experiencing a fair or unfair distribution of resources? Or are non-theoretical emotional expectations enough to generate a social system of reciprocity and then fairness?

40. See William Saletan, "Mind Makes Right," *Slate*, March 31, 2007. Ralph Adolphs, professor of psychology and neuroscience at the California Institute of Technology in Pasadena, has published many studies that show brain correlations in emotional and cognitive processing. His lab is very active in exploring neural substrates

for moral reasoning/emoting. See his website for an extensive bibliography of papers: http://www.emotion.caltech.edu/.

41. See Charles Darwin's *Descent of Man*, especially the discussion of "moral sense" in the "General Summary and Conclusion," chapter XXI, in *Darwin: A Norton Critical Edition* (Norton, 1979).

42. Arranged marriages in South Asia, Africa, and the Middle East are still dominant. Over 90 percent of weddings in India are still arranged. Parents and/or matchmakers look to maximize the welfare of the entire multigenerational family by finding prosperous and resourceful spousal matches. The offspring of such a union will be the obvious first recipients of a successful new bond, but the extended family will also find significant indirect benefits.

43. Special thanks to an anonymous reviewer, who helped me to better articulate this point about Hume.

Chapter Three

1. Biologists Peter J. Richerson and Robert Boyd have produced a series of compelling articles and books, arguing that instinctual tribalism (which we share with other social primates) was united with unique "group selection" mechanisms that favored functional large-scale institutions. Dedication to more abstract large-scale groups always competes with tighter tribal instincts, but human culture has many "workaround" solutions to strengthen the wider group allegiance, even ensure sacrifices to larger group interests. These work-arounds include the personal charisma of leaders and the uses of ideology (the exploitation of big-brained symbol systems) to inform and enforce socially stabilizing hierarchies and stratifications. Social insects like ants don't need these work-around cultural evolution mechanisms because vast numbers of colony members are literally "family." So, kin selection is probably enough to explain much of their social cohesion. My own discussion, in what follows, of a cultural grid of egalitarian fairness might be seen as part of this co-evolution thesis, which avoids reducing humans to the simple "human nature" theses we find in sociobiology and rational choice cost-benefit approaches. Despite the counterbalancing of human ideology, the tribal instincts are, I believe, older and stronger, and represent a real limit on the size of group membership. See Peter J. Richerson and Robert Boyd, "Complex Societies: The Evolutionary Origins of a Crude Superorganism," *Human Nature* 10, no. 3 (1999): 253–89.

2. Rembrandt is just the most famous of the Dutch Golden Age painters, but group portraiture was ubiquitous during this time. See Frans Hals's (c. 1581–1666) group portrait from 1641, *Regents of the Company of St. Elizabeth* (Hals is also noteworthy because of his famous portrait of René Descartes), or Ferdinand Bol's *The Officers of the Guild of Wine Merchants* (c. 1659), or the group portraits of Bartholomeus van der Helst (1613–1670).

3. Competing interpretations of Rembrandt's famous *Night Watch* (1642) are discussed in Michael Hatt and Charlotte Klonk, *Art History: A Critical Introduction to Its Methods* (Manchester University Press, 2006), chap. 5. Hatt and Klonk assess whether the Dutch group portraits can be accurately said to promote egalitarian values.

4. See Arthur Lovejoy's classic book *The Great Chain of Being: A Study of the History of an Idea* (Harvard University Press, 1936).

5. Descartes, in his *Principia*, discards qualitative differences in natural philosophy. "For I freely acknowledge that I recognize no matter in corporeal things apart from that which the geometers call quantity, and take as the object of their demonstrations, i.e. that to which every kind of division, shape and motion is applicable." Part II, thesis 64, *The Principles of Philosophy*, in *The Philosophical Writings of Descartes: Vol. I* (Cambridge University Press, 1985).

6. For an excellent discussion of the various attempts to marry Newtonian universalism to emerging social science and humanities interests in the Enlightenment era, see Stephen Toulmin, *Cosmopolis: The Hidden Agenda of Modernity* (University of Chicago Press, 1992).

7. True emotivist ethics emerges out of the logical positivism movement in the early twentieth century but harkens back to Hume's view that emotions are not subject to rational dispute or resolution. Positivism saw ethical claims (as well as religious and aesthetic claims) as incapable of logical proof and empirical corroboration, so they deemed ethics to be an expression of subjective emotion. They promptly roped off the whole domain and proceeded to ignore it. The earlier sentiment philosophers, like Hume and Smith, were still optimistic that a systematic and normative management of emotions was attainable and advisable for large-scale social progress.

8. David Hume, *A Treatise on Human Nature* (Oxford University Press, 2000), bk. II, part III.

9. Adam Smith, *Theory of Moral Sentiments* (1759) (Prometheus Books, 2000) part I, sec. I, chap. V.

10. Jeremy Bentham, *The Principles of Morals and Legislation* (1789) (Prometheus Books, 1988), 1.

11. Utilitarians saw themselves as improving upon the sentiment theories of Hume and Smith, by breaking down the emotions to their atomic elements—pain and pleasure. In this, the utilitarians are early forerunners of the later behaviorism school of psychology. This reductionist utilitarian move may have brought the ethical project closer to the mathematized Newtonian ideal, but at a great cost. My own view is that Hume and Smith were closer to the mark in their consideration of more complex emotions (e.g., sympathy, compassion, revenge, shame, etc.). As my earlier explication of a biological CARE system demonstrates, affective systems can be very sophisticated and irreducibly tied to specific content in the social life of the organism. Pain and pleasure play a role in biological attachment, for example, but they woefully underdetermine the parent-child emotional bond.

12. Kant offers three different formulations of the categorical imperative. The first formulation is famous, but the others are important too. The second formulation is "Act in such a way that you treat humanity, whether in your own person or in the person of any other, always at the same time as an end and never merely as a means to an end." And the final formation is "Every rational being must so act as if he were through his maxim always a legislating member in the universal kingdom of ends." *Grounding for the Metaphysics of Morals*, trans. James Ellington (Hackett, 1993), 43.

13. There are many arguments against Kant's ethics in general and the lying case in particular, including the fact that language only needs partial reliability to function quite well as a communication system. Also, as many philosophers have pointed out, application of the universalizing categorical imperative to most other mundane dilemmas (e.g., should I do my laundry at midnight on Monday?) also leads to weird moral violations. Jean-Paul Sartre also demonstrates the vapid nature of the categorical imperative when applied to concrete dilemmas, in his essay "Existentialism Is a Humanism." But I am not interested here in detailing the many counter-arguments to Kant's philosophy. I am obviously much more sympathetic to the tradition that grounds ethics in emotion.

14. Hume continues here, "It is sufficient, if the whole plan or scheme be necessary to the support of civil society, and if the balance of good, in the main, do thereby preponderate much above that of evil." Harold I. Brown analyzes this passage—originally from appendix III of Hume, *Enquiries*, ed. L. A. Selby-Bigge (Oxford University Press, 1975)—in order to contrast it with the more improvisational techniques of rational "judgment." I'm in agreement with Brown, who thinks that science itself doesn't even follow the naively formalist rationality that it officially praises. See his *Rationality* (Routledge, 1990), 305.

15. Some have suggested that the grid has been a long time coming, foreshadowed and even given a first draft in ancient Greek democracy. Ideas of democratic equality— one person, one vote—didn't have to wait for the Enlightenment but already existed in our ancestral Athens. I don't share this view of history—at the very least, it needs important caveats.

Ancient Greek democracy is much closer to its tribal parentage than we usually admit. Yes, the people (*demos*) technically ruled the city-state, but the people had to be citizens in order to vote. Being a citizen was more tribal than we often realize. Women were not allowed to vote, nor were slaves or foreigners. A man could vote if he had already completed military training or if he owned property (although this last criterion was not well enforced). To be a citizen, you had to be the son of an Athenian, and Pericles tightened the criterion to insist that both parents be Athenian (thereby excluding sons of Athenian fathers and foreign mothers).

It's true that early democracy widened the parameters of the tribe—giving voice and influence beyond the usual oligarchies and tyrannies, but it was no grid. Even the Enlightenment version was universal in its pretensions but more tribal in practice. Many historians have chronicled the hypocritical exclusivity of eighteenth-century human rights policy. But my objective in this little historical sketch is to show how the promise of egalitarianism was born in this period, and how the subsequent two centuries were attempts to slowly make good on that promise.

16. Jonathan Haidt has been researching the psychological aspects of moral intuitions and convictions. His empirical data reveal some of the interesting cognitive and affective psychodynamics at work underneath the American liberal and conservative tension. See Haidt and Craig Joseph, "The Moral Mind: How Five Sets of Innate Intuitions Guide the Development of Many Culture-Specific Virtues, and Perhaps Even Modules," in *The Innate Mind: Foundations and the Future*, vol. 3, ed. P. Carruthers, S. Laurence, and S. Stich (Oxford University Press, 2008).

17. I am from Chicago, a city notorious for corruption with a long history of dubious ethics. As I write this, Rahm Emanuel has become the first new mayor after Richard M. Daley's twenty-two-year reign (one year more than his long-serving father, Richard J. Daley). Nepotism was a way of life for the Daley family, but the often-raised corruption charge never fully stuck on Richard M. Daley. Daley's brother Michael's law firm handled many zoning cases involving the city of Chicago, his other brother John sold insurance to city contractors, and his nephew Robert Vanecko signed many high-end city-related service contracts and development deals. Family-based patronage has been a long-standing way of life in my hometown.

18. The major complaint that we level, regarding violation of public trust, is that the alderman is using public money—not his own money—to pay his brother's company. This seems like a reasonable complaint, but the alderman is not stealing public money and giving it to his brother. He is preferentially hiring his brother to do a job for which public funds are earmarked. The money is already going to build a new youth center. And the brother's company is in fact working hard to build the center—provide the service. Did the alderman bend bidding rules that are designed to ensure the fair chance of unrelated contractors? Yes, he did. But unless he is stealing money somewhere in this scenario (and I can't see that), then he owes more to his brother than the stranger contractors. Does he owe more to his constituents—being a public servant—than to his brother? That depends on more details. If the brother is an incompetent contractor and might potentially build a youth center that fails to serve the constituents (or worse, injures them), then the safety of strangers outweighs the financial advantage of the inept brother. But most cases do not involve such jeopardy, and the nepotism itself is not intrinsically wrong.

19. See Aristotle, *Nicomachean Ethics*, trans. W. D. Ross, in *The Basic Works of Aristotle*, ed. Richard McKeon (Random House, 1941), bk. 8.

20. Philosopher David Annis has argued that special duties actually *make* a relationship into a friendship. See his "The Meaning, Value, and Duties of Friendship," *American Philosophical Quarterly* 24 (1987): 349–56.

21. The near worship of mathematical rationality in the Enlightenment was not an arbitrary assumption. The very real advances in physics, astronomy, and chemistry were staggering and inspirational. But the rule-based hypothetico-deductive model failed as a one-size-fits-all methodology.

22. Bernard Williams famously raised many objections to the theoretical ethics of Kantian and utilitarian philosophies. I am indebted to the spirit of his many critiques. He led the charge that theorists like Kant and Rawls asked something impossible of us. These theorists, Williams argues, ask us to consider the world from no point of view. Contrary to the formalists, the goal of ethics is not that I should become a "servant of the world." That's too abstract and irrelevant to my actual idiosyncratic life. But in place of rule-governed theoretical ethics, Williams posits a kind of "methodological intuition ism." We find our way through moral dilemmas and challenges by *intuiting* the right thing. This intuitionism is not mystical, but a way of denying the a priori and algorithmic methods of theoretical rationality. While I share Williams's general dissatisfaction, my own "solution" departs from his. I think Aristotelian notions of practical reason (problem solving without certainty or even first principles) are sufficient to guide us

without appeals to mathematical logic or intuitionism. See Bernard Williams, *Making Sense of Humanity and Other Philosophical Essays, 1982–1993* (Cambridge University Press, 1995).

23. This discussion of friendship is drawn from Aristotle, *Nicomachean Ethics*, bks. VIII, IX.

24. See ibid, bk. VIII, chap. 11.

25. See Frank Calabrese Jr. with Keith Zimmerman, Kent Zimmerman, and Paul Pompian, *Operation Family Secrets: How a Mobster's Son and the FBI Brought Down Chicago's Murderous Crime Family* (Broadway Books, 2011).

26. I am very much indebted to Stephen Toulmin's career-long indictment that modern philosophy abandoned practical reason in favor of theoretical frames of meaning. And I agree with his call to reintroduce the contextual nature—historical, literary, and even emotional context—of knowledge and meaning (without the typical relativism maneuvers). The quote is taken from his *Return to Reason* (Harvard University Press, 2001), 111. In addition to Toulmin's critiques, Barry Schwartz and Kenneth Sharpe's *Practical Wisdom* (Riverhead, 2010) is an excellent sustained application of Aristotelian judgment to contemporary social issues. They demonstrate the various problems of our modern tendency to use bloodless rule-based rationality in areas like medicine, law, and education.

27. Toulmin, *Return to Reason*, 130.

28. Aristotle, *Nicomachean Ethics*, bk. I.3.

29. See Seneca, *Ad Lucilium epistulae morales* vol. 2 (Loeb Classical Library, Harvard University Press, 1962), epistle LXXXI, "On Benefits."

30. The actual track record of *applied* egalitarianism is not very impressive. Toulmin points out, "Despite all the subtlety and depth they display in abstract general terms, the conclusions of a book like John Rawl's *Theory of Justice* provide no effective criteria for settling real-life disputes in actual cases." Toulmin, *Return to Reason*, 124.

Chapter Four

1. See Plato, *Republic*, trans. Benjamin Jowett (Vintage Classic, 1991), bk. IX.

2. Hesiod, *Works and Days* (Hackett, 1993), 32.

3. Some thoroughly enlightened progressive parents will no doubt scoff at my carrot-and-stick philosophy of early moral training. Some parents try to reason with their toddlers and think that cool-headed talk alone is enough to curb behavior. But a mother who reasons with her child that he's "hurt her feelings" or done something "unfair" is demonstrating through emotional body language and expressions that she is upset at the child, and the child will reorganize his behavior because he fears the loss of love. His feelings are being manipulated, albeit to good ends, just as in the other more deceptive cases. Many contemporary parents congratulate themselves on the humane wisdom of the "time-out." But for toddlers, being separated from their loved ones is a strong violation of their affective desire to belong, to be with, to be safe. I'm not interested in debating parenting styles, but only in showing how even the most cerebral parenting persuades kids with *affects* like fear and love, not with argumentation.

4. Mirror neurons were first discovered by a team of Italian neurologists in the early 1990s and are commonly believed to be one of the most important recent discover-

ies in neuroscience. One of the original researchers, Dr. Vittorio Gallese, has written (together with Maxim I. Stamenov) a fairly comprehensive story of the discovery and implications, called *Mirror Neurons and the Evolution of Brain and Language* (John Benjamins, 2002). I adopt his helpful term "shared manifold," which he articulates in "The 'Shared Manifold' Hypothesis: From Mirror Neurons to Empathy," *Journal of Consciousness Studies* 8 (2001): 33–50.

5. See Jean Piaget, *The Psychology of the Child* (Basic Books, 1972), sec. 4.

6. Limbic values are the kinds of natural emotional responses that we find in our mammal brains, below the neocortical level. "Values," here, refers more to the positive or negative valence of a stimulus. In psychology this experience of positive (attraction) valence or negative (aversion) valence precedes conscious thought. Recall that in chapter 2, I detailed how one of these limbic based systems works—the CARE system of mammalian bonding (articulated best in Dr. Jaak Panksepp's affective neuroscience). But CARE is only one of these emotional systems, and art narratives (even kids' movies) can tap into many other limbic values.

7. This lesson and the guidelines are taken from a recent Texas elementary school curriculum document at http://schools.cms.k12.nc.us/beverlywoodsES/Documents/ Janjustice.pdf. They've drawn the egg "experiment" from Jaime Miller's *10-Minute Life Lessons* (Harper Paperbacks, 1998).

8. The 2004 manual *Diversity and Equity in Early Childhood Training in Europe* is produced by the DECET Network (www.decet.org) in The Hague, the Netherlands. The principal investigators include Anke van Keulen, Dominique Malleval, Miriam Mony, Colette Murray, and Michel Vendenbroeck.

9. My argument here draws on the research of psychologists Melanie Killen, Heidi McGlothlin, and Alexandra Henning. See their "Explicit Judgments and Implicit Bias," in *Intergroup Attitudes and Relations in Childhood through Adulthood*, ed. Sheri R. Levy and Melanie Killen (Oxford University Press, 2008). Also see the earlier study by Naomi Struch and Shalom H. Schwartz, "Intergroup Aggression: Its Predictors and Distinctness from In-Group Bias," *Journal of Personality and Social Psychology* 56, no. 3 (1989): 364–73.

10. Psychologists Killen, McGlothlin, and Henning, "Explicit Judgments and Implicit Bias," articulate the problems inherent in the forced-choice method. "[A] child who assigns the trait 'nice' to the picture card that looks like the self (ingroup) may do so to associate a positive trait with the self; this decision may not reflect anything about the child's outgroup attitude. Conversely, assigning a negative trait to a picture card reflecting a member of the outgroup may be a result of avoiding associating a negative trait with the ingroup rather than as a reflection of a negative view of the outgroup category" (128). This is just one of the ways that confounds the earlier findings.

11. This new vision, called the "social domain model," is articulated in Judith Smetana, "Social Domain Theory: Consistencies and Variations in Children's Moral and Social Judgments," in *Handbook of Moral Development*, ed. M. Killen and J. Smetana (Lawrence Erlbaum Associates, 2006).

12. Killen, McGlothlin, and Henning, "Explicit Judgments and Implicit Bias," 129.

13. See Henri Tajfel, *Social Identity and Intergroup Relations* (Cambridge University Press, 2010).

14. Cicero, *De Amicitia* (Loeb Classical Library, Harvard University Press, 1923), chap. 5.

15. See Nietzsche, *Thus Spoke Zarathustra* (Cambridge University Press, 2006), part I, "On Chastity."

16. See Alexis de Tocqueville's 1850 letter to Nassau William Senior, "Preference of égalité to liberty," in *Correspondence and Conversations of Alexis de Tocqueville with Nassau William Senior from 1834 to 1859*, vol. 1, ed. M. C. M. Simpson (Henry S. King and Co., 1873), 94.

17. Aquinas, *Summa Theologica* (BiblioBazaar, 2009), question 36, "Of Envy."

18. See Susan J. Matt, "Children's Envy and the Emergence of the Modern Consumer Ethic, 1890–1930," *Journal of Social History* 36, no. 2 (2002): 297.

19. Ibid.

20. Ivan Illich, in his *Tools for Conviviality* (Harper and Row, 1973), 47, writes: "In a consumer society there are inevitably two kinds of slaves: the prisoners of addiction and the prisoners of envy."

21. For an interesting discussion of the revenge component in justice, see David P. Barash and Judith Eve Lipton, "Why We Needed Bin Laden Dead: Revenge as a Biological Imperative," *Chronicle Review*, May 5, 2011, 814–15.

22. *The Autobiography of Michel de Montaigne* (David R. Godine, 1999), 318.

23. If egalitarianism and other causes like environmentalism are substitutions for religion—a way of validating certain emotions—then we might expect to find other secular surrogates for guilt, envy, and indignation. Our tendencies to sin, repent, and generally indulge in self-cruelty can be seen cropping up in our obsessions about health and fitness, for example. Struggling with our weight (diet and relapse) has risen above the other deadly sins to take a dominant position in our secular self-persecution. But our resentful aggression still manages to find some occasional pathways to the external world. As successfully socialized citizens, we may not be able to punch the people we want to punch in real life, but we can turn some of our aggression outward at the reprobates of TV land. What a joyful hatred we can all feel at the Octomom, Lindsay Lohan, Charlie Sheen, and more importantly political nepotists who engage in cronyism. Television provides us with a parade of thoroughly cleansing moral outrages. And more of this kind of indignation, previously reserved for religious condemnation, can be seen everywhere on the screens and airwaves of the twenty-four-hour "news" cycle. Large segments of the news seem calculated to facilitate the catharsis of our built-up resentment. Daytime talk shows and reality shows seem similarly designed to elicit our righteous anger—which in the case of celebrity TV comes to rescue our painful sense of envy. This envy is caused by a procession of "bling" and celebrity lifestyle privilege. These emotions form the other side of the religious coin—in addition to the masochism of guilt, we can vent our aggression outwardly (like a crowd at a witch drowning) as long as it's justified by piety or the defense of fairness.

24. See Jonathan Haidt and Craig Joseph, "The Moral Mind: How Five Sets of Innate Intuitions Guide the Development of Many Culture-Specific Virtues, and Perhaps Even Modules," in *The Innate Mind: Foundations and the Future*, vol. 3, ed. P. Carruthers, S. Laurence, and S. Stich (Oxford University Press, 2008).

25. Jan-Willem van Prooijen, "Fairness Judgments: Genuine Morality or Disguised

Egocentrism?," *Inquisitive Mind*, no. 4, http://beta.in-mind.org/issue-4/fairness-judgments-genuine-morality-or-disguised-egocentrism.

26. In chapter 2, I introduced a bio-psychological idea called "homeostasis" that describes the well-functioning equilibrium of a system, in this case the brain. I described how family bonding restores pleasurable homeostatic chemistry in us, so we tend to seek it out. So, too, if you've been mistreated or even feel like you've been wronged, you get physiologically imbalanced with increased cortisone levels, hypertension, lowered sex drive, and so on. Perhaps our drive for fair redistribution of goods is partly a veiled attempt to recalibrate our own discomfort levels, our own homeostasis.

27. See William A. Henry's hilarious and insightful screed *In Defensive of Elitism* (Doubleday, 1994), chap. 8, for an analysis of the Clinton case, but also for a general articulation of the "merit-based" critique of egalitarianism.

28. James Poniewozik, "Six Thumbs—Up," *Time*, May 9, 2011, 58.

29. See Joseph Tobin, Yeh Hsueh, and Mayumi Karasawa, *Preschool in Three Different Cultures: Revisited* (University of Chicago Press, 2009).

30. Steve Salerno, "Positively Misguided," *Skeptic* 14, no. 4 (2009): 30–37.

Chapter Five

1. Christina Hoff Sommers, "Filial Morality," *Journal of Philosophy* 83, no. 8 (1986): 439.

2. Translations of *Xiao Jing* are by Feng Xin-ming, 2008. See www.tsoidug.org.

3. Ibid., chap. 2.

4. "The ruler of the state does not dare to bully the wifeless and the widowed, so how can he bully the officers and people? Thus he gets the affection of all the families, with which he serves his ancestral lords." Ibid., chap. 8.

5. Yong Ho, "Cultural Insights," in *Beginner's Chinese* (Hippocrene Books, 2010), 48.

6. *Xiao Jing*, chap. 9

7. It may sound strange to refer to the "Chinese district" of Shanghai—like saying, "I lived in the American district of Chicago." But Shanghai has been so cosmopolitan for so long (even once carved into French and British territories), that the Chinese ethnicity of my neighborhood is worth mention. I did not live in the renowned international melting pot of downtown Shanghai—the skyscraper-filled, Vegas-looking spectacle you see on TV. I lived in a Chinese neighborhood that just happened to be located on the far west side of the otherwise bustling Shanghai metropolis.

8. You might protest and claim that Chairman Mao gave the Chinese people an ideological taste of a leveled equal society, but in truth he only reversed the usual pyramid by temporarily putting the worker on top. And these days the revolution has evaporated in the midst of a new capitalist hierarchy. If Chairman Mao saw present-day Shanghai, he would start spinning in his Plexiglas case in Beijing.

9. There are lots of reasons why this nepotistic world of bias is problematic. For example, people get stuck in arranged marriages, or they spend their lives studying and then working in jobs their parents picked for them. I do not deny the abuses that sometimes infect nepotism. But the positive aspects of widespread tribalism are underappreciated by many Westerners.

10. Meir Statman, "Local Ethics in a Global World," *Financial Analysts Journal* 63, no. 3 (2007): 33.

11. See the preface of Amartya Sen's magisterial study, *The Idea of Justice* (Harvard University Press, 2009).

12. I agree with this general point about the Buddha, and I explore the egalitarianism of Buddhism in three of my own books. See *Why I Am a Buddhist* (Hampton Roads, 2010), *The Gods Drink Whiskey* (2005), and *Buddha: A Beginner's Guide* (Hampton Roads, 2008).

13. Despite being born in India, the Buddha's unique intellectual revolution did not significantly impact the subsequent Indian psyche because Buddhism was reabsorbed into hierarchical Hinduism (e.g., Gotama was reinterpreted as an incarnation of Vishnu), and then the remaining vestiges of it were pushed out by the eventual rise of Islam.

14. See A. K. Ramanujan's essay "Is There an Indian Way of Thinking?," in *India through Hindu Categories*, ed. McKim Marriot (Sage, 1990). Ramanujan's essay has greatly influenced my thinking in this section. I want to thank my colleague Joan Erdman for exposing me to Ramanujan's important work.

15. Ibid.

16. Ramanujan explains, "Even space and time, the universal contexts, the Kantian imperatives, are in India not uniform and neutral, but have properties, varying specific densities, that affect those who dwell in them." He goes on to remark, "Time too does not come in uniform units: certain hours of the day, certain days of the week, etc., are auspicious or inauspicious." Ibid., 51.

17. See Alan Roland, *In Search of Self in India and Japan* (Princeton University Press, 1989), and his *Cultural Pluralism and Psychoanalysis* (Routledge, 1996).

18. Michael Paterniti, "The Man Who Sailed His House," *GQ*, October 2011, 206.

19. Two objections to my praise of Asian favoritism might be raised here. One, which I'll call the "weak objection," is that we cannot disentangle the good aspects of Indian filial piety from the bad aspects—like caste prejudices. The weak objection says that favoritist cultures are heavily mixed amalgams of positive and negative cultural commitments and can't be sifted, excavated, or adapted by our culture for useful strategies. The baggage of history makes such borrowing nigh impossible. To this weak objection, I hold out not just the optimism that cultures can learn from each other, but also the extensive historical record of such cultural borrowing, adaptation, and fusion. Yes, if we borrowed more Asian values of filial piety in the West, we would surely change them in the translation and we would import some unwanted aspects too, but it's exactly this kind of "values immigration" that accompanies, for example, every migration of religion to a new country (e.g., Christianity was extracted and transplanted repeatedly from one country to another, as was Islam, as was democracy, as was communism, as was Beatlemania). Secondly, the "strong objection" looks something like this: Asian values, and therefore Asian countries, are uniquely suited for autocratic control, subjugation of citizenry, and the inevitable compromise of human rights. It's as hard to falsify this bold claim as it is to prove it, but I'm clearly not sympathetic. It rings to my ear more like Western hype than truth. Some have blamed the acquiescent nature of Buddhism, for example, on the rise of Maoist repression in China and the

tyranny of Pol Pot in Cambodia. Such a strong objection toward my view would assert that Asian tribalism contributed to the disastrous social experiments, famines, and mass murders in twentieth-century Asia. I'm doubtful. It seems more likely to me that Confucian tribalism, for example, would have been an excellent buffer against the excesses of Maoist egalitarian ideology. Confucian filial tribalism was exactly the sort of bourgeois value system that could have protected families against the overreaching "science" of the state party. Asian tribalism failed to protect against autocracy because it was systematically and explicitly rooted out. Blaming the Asian social disasters of the late twentieth century on tribal favoritism is convenient for some Western ideologues, but not more true for that convenience.

20. Interestingly, Plato makes a similar argument in the *Republic* (bk. V) for the superiority of communal families over nuclear families. And the American Oneida Community tried to put communal families into practice in nineteenth-century New York.

21. See Aristotle's discussion of "Temperance" in *Nicomachean Ethics*, ed. Lesley Brown, trans. David Ross (Oxford University Press, 2009), bk. III, chap. 12.

22. Obviously, political structures are not the same as family structures, and power generalizations from one domain cannot easily transfer to another. But we also can't make neat divisions of "public" and "private" values, and just hope for them to conveniently pass each other in the night. I think political scientist Samuel P. Huntington—famous for his "clash of civilizations" thesis—was wrong about a lot of things, but he, too, grasped the relevance and interconnection of family dynamics to political dynamics. He thought it was unlikely for Confucian cultures to become democracies. See Huntington, *The Clash of Civilizations and the Remaking of World Order* (Touchstone, 1996), chap. 9. Democracies, he argues, require *individualism*, and the Confucian family-based subjugation of individuality to group interests renders democracy impossible. Political scientist Francis Fukuyama has counter-argued this incompatibility view and claims that there are ways for Confucian values and democratic values to find common ground. See Fukuyama, "Confucianism and Democracy," *Journal of Democracy* 6, no. 2 (1995): 20–33.

23. The real reason for placing power-sharing checks on autocrats is not because they cannot lead benevolently, but because "bad eggs" (unethical rulers) can't be withdrawn (can't be gotten rid of) without some representational mechanisms.

24. I want to avoid a problem that philosophers sometimes make. It is not enough to point out the "logical possibility" of disentangling centralized power and corruption. One must empirically study the history of such power distributions and evaluate them in the arena of human tendencies, not just logical possibilities. Egalitarians will point to the "real world" to trump the claims of logical possibility. And yet real-world analysis does not clearly support the Western assumption that democracy reduces corruption. Using data from NGO Transparency International and the World Bank, social scientist Kang Xiaoguang analyzed the relationship between democracy, economic development, corruption index, and poverty index for eighteen countries. Xiaoguang, "Confucianization: A Future in the Tradition," *Social Research: An International Quarterly of the Social Sciences* 73, no. 1 (Spring 2006). The data reveals that there is no statistical evidence for the claim that democracy reduces corruption (nor does democracy correlate well with economic growth). More surprising for egalitarians might be the fact that the

Gini coefficient (the degree of economic inequality) does not correlate with political democracy. Economic disparity between rich and poor is approximately the same, for example, in the United States and China, according to 2009 Gini calculations. More centralized governments—like one-party China, parliamentary republics as in Europe, or even parliamentary monarchies like Thailand—do not automatically produce more corruption or inequality than egalitarian democracies.

25. American nepotism in the workplace is carefully examined in Bridgette Kaye Harder, "On Nepotism: An Examination of Kinship, Merit and Perceptions of Fairness" (MA thesis, DePaul University, 2006), 2. Harder's survey of the research (or more accurately, lack of research) on nepotism is fascinating, as is her discussion of the complex ties between perceptions of fairness and workplace organizational justice. My discussion in this section is indebted to her helpful research. Also see Karen L. Vinton, "Nepotism: An Interdisciplinary Model," *Family Business Review* 11, no. 4 (1998): 297–303.

26. See D. R. Laker and M. L. Williams, "Nepotism's Effect on Employee Satisfaction and Organizational Commitment: An Empirical Study," *International Journal of Human Resources Development and Management* 3, no. 3 (2003): 191–202.

27. The infamous "Hutu 10 Commandments" propaganda article was published in the anti-Tutsi newspaper *Kangura* in 1990. It lists a frightening set of hateful rules that fueled the eventual genocide, including the warning to never trust a Tutsi woman (do not marry across tribal lines) and the command: "The Hutu should stop having mercy on the Tutsi."

28. See my *On Monsters: An Unnatural History of Our Worst Fears* (Oxford University Press, 2009), chap. 14, for a fuller discussion of the demonizing ideologies that accompany xenophobia between diverse groups.

29. See Jared Diamond's compelling analysis of the Rwandan genocide in *Collapse: How Societies Choose to Fail or Succeed* (Penguin, 2005), part 4.

30. Ibid.

31. Frank Snowden shows, in *Before Color Prejudice: The Ancient View of Blacks* (Harvard University Press, 1991), that previous eras carved up in-groups, but not along color lines. Us-and-them group dynamics in the ancient Mediterranean tended to carve up along language and cultural lines, not skin color or race.

Chapter Six

1. Interestingly, I may or may not be Jewish. My mother was adopted and has little information about her birth parents, except the last name of her biological mother—which looks like a Jewish surname. If the single criterion "born of a Jewish mother" applies, then I might qualify.

2. See Nicholas Wade, "Y Chromosome Bears Witness to Story of Jewish Diaspora," *New York Times*, May 9, 2000.

3. In 1992 education professor Alvin Wolf surveyed American history textbooks between the 1940s and the 1980s. As one might expect, minority representation was notably poor and unbalanced from the 1940s to the early 1970s. Starting in the 1970s, however, the tides turned somewhat and minority representation expanded considerably, but also took on the expression of moral high ground. In an attempt to make up

for earlier unfairness, a kind of "textual affirmative action" emerged in history textbooks. Wolf cites scholars N. Glazer and R. Ueda in suggesting that many textbooks of
the 1970s and 1980s had begun to romanticize minorities in American history. "Along
the same line, after reviewing excerpts from a few books on how Mexicans were poorly
treated in the eighteenth and nineteenth centuries, Glazer and Ueda write: 'Once again
one wonders whether a crude dualism—in this case pernicious Anglos and exploited
Mexicans—gives the right balance to history.' That white people have been villains and
minorities have been victims is part of America's history, unfortunately. But some books
may be bending too far, Glazer and Ueda caution, in reducing history to exploiters and
exploited, an oversimplified view that should be avoided. These commentators call for
balance and completeness in history books. Their concerns raise cautions for educa-
tors, authors, publishers, and adoptions committees." See Wolf's interesting survey
"Minorities in U.S. History Textbooks, 1945–1985," Clearing House 65, no. 5 (May/
June 1992): 291.

4. See Scott Shaffer, "When a Gay Judge Rules on Gay Rights," Morning Edition, KQED Public Broadcasting, June 13, 2011, http://www.kqed.org/news/
story/2011/06/13/57300/when_a_gay_judge_rules_on_gay_rights?category=u.s.

5. The Johnson quote is taken from an excellent article by William M. Chace,
"Affirmative Inaction," American Scholar (Winter 2011): 20. I'm indebted to Chace
throughout my discussion of affirmative action, for his clear and nuanced assessment of
the policy.

6. I am indebted to my friend Glenn Curran, Esq., for walking me through the
legal evolution of affirmative action, and for our many general discussions of law and
philosophy.

7. Chace, "Affirmative Inaction," 26.

8. There may be very good arguments for maintaining preferential treatment for
African Americans specifically—and I think there are good arguments—but they will
probably need definitive detachment from current affirmative action. Since African
Americans continue to be underrepresented in today's universities—despite an all-time-
high representation of non-white students—some policies should probably return to the
language and logic of reparation (rather than just equal opportunity). If not reparation
(which is harder to justify as we get further away from historical mistreatment), then
perhaps a new criteria of "low-income" status would obliquely raise educational opportunities for African Americans and Latinos (and avoid the wide-net problem of color
diversity).

9. Richard Kahlenberg, "Is Affirmative Action Headed Back to the Supreme
Court?," Chronicle of Higher Education, June 21, 2011.

10. In schools we have a microcosm tension between two competing national
values: egalitarian community and meritocratic excellence. As I mentioned in the first
chapter, these two values are often characterized in the rhetoric of fairness—even
though they often cancel each other out. Affirmative action wades into this messy
swamp of American values and inevitably confuses our national intuitions further.

11. Notice here that "encouraging diversity" is often entwined in the fairness debate,
but philosophically it seems unrelated. Having diversity in a population is defensible
from broader ethical notions of the good society—diversity gives interpersonal perspec-

tive, global awareness, greater tolerance, new idea banks of creativity, cross-fertilization of culture, and even biological advantage because of genetic variation in interbreeding. None of this requires or benefits from fairness considerations.

12. A recent Princeton study analyzed the records of more than 100,000 applicants to three highly selective private universities. "They found that being an African American candidate was worth, on average, an additional 230 SAT points on the 1600-point scale and that being Hispanic was worth an additional 185 points, but that being an Asian-American candidate warranted the loss, on average, of 50 SAT points." Chace, "Affirmative Inaction," 23.

13. Thomas Sowell, *Affirmative Action Around the World: An Empirical Study* (Yale University Press, 2004).

14. I'm not a fan of Plato's utopian political philosophy, but Plato raises an important point in the course of his project. In book IV of the *Republic*, Socrates' friends stop him in the middle of his utopian construction, noticing that some classes of people have a harder road than others. Warriors, for example, don't get the nice houses and fattening foods that other groups might enjoy. Plato responds to this by reminding them that the healthy state is totally different than a state in which all people have equal pleasures. "Suppose that we were painting a statue, and some one came up to us and said, Why do you not put the most beautiful colors on the most beautiful parts of the body—the eyes ought to be purple, but you have made them black—to him we might fairly answer, Sir, you would not surely have us beautify the eyes to such a degree that they are no longer eyes; consider rather whether, by giving this and the other features their due proportion, we make the whole beautiful." Plato, *Republic*, trans. Benjamin Jowett (Vintage Classic, 1991), bk. IV.

15. See Lance Lochner and Enrico Moretti, "The Effect of Education on Crime: Evidence from Prison Inmates, Arrests, and Self-Reports," *American Economic Review* 94, no. 1 (2004): 155–89.

16. See Peter Singer, *The Expanding Circle: Ethics, Evolution, and Moral Progress* (Princeton University Press, 2011), 119.

17. Ibid.

18. See Kwame Anthony Appiah's excellent critique of Singer in his *Cosmopolitanism: Ethics in a World of Strangers* (Norton, 2007), chap. 10.

19. Jeremy Rifkin, *The Empathic Civilization: The Race to Global Consciousness in a World of Crisis* (Tarcher/Penguin, 2009).

20. Ibid., 616.

21. See Robin Dunbar, *How Many Friends Does One Person Need?: Dunbar's Number and Other Evolutionary Quirks* (Harvard University Press, 2010).

22. See Isaiah Berlin, "Pursuit of the Ideal," in *The Crooked Timber of Humanity* (Princeton University Press, 1998).

23. See Isaiah Berlin, "My Intellectual Path," in his *The Power of Ideas*, ed. Henry Hardy (Princeton University Press, 1998).

24. Ibid., 10.

25. See my discussion of "reasonable favoritism" in chapter 3 as a model of how nuanced ethical judgments can proceed in the absence of fixed absolute rules.

26. I'm indebted to Nicholas Kristof's use of Deng's famous quote, in his excellent

study of Isaiah Berlin. Kristof, "On Isaiah Berlin," *New York Review of Books*, February 25, 2010, 26.

27. Communitarianism is an ideological movement for which I have some sympathy. The communitarians take the Rawlsian notion of fairness as problematic, and they tend to stress community (especially family) over individualism. In all this, I am in agreement. Still, many communitarians are overly optimistic and utopian about harmonizing the competing interests of groups. They often adopt a hopeful view that communities are themselves egalitarian oases of respect and that there will one day be a grand-scale harmony of currently conflicting communities. I'm rather more pessimistic than this.

28. In *Practical Wisdom* (Riverhead 2010), Barry Schwartz and Kenneth Sharpe tell a heartbreaking story about a robbery case, presided over by Philadelphia Judge Lois Forer. The extenuating circumstances of the case led Judge Forer to violate the a priori sentencing rules and dispense a more just punishment to the offender, who had a family that depended on him and had no previous criminal record. The offender had been gainfully employed, paying for his daughter to attend a parochial school, when he was suddenly laid off. In desperation, he used a toy gun to rob fifty dollars. When the prosecutor learned of the lighter sentence, he appealed and forced an uncritical application of the relevant mandatory sentencing rule, effectively ruining the lives of the offender and his family. The punishment, five years in prison, bore no just or proper relation to the unique aspects of the case. If the judge had been allowed to actually *judge* the case, rather than be bound up by inappropriate rules, then justice might have had a chance. These kinds of cases demonstrate not just the *possibility* of non-arbitrary reasonable judgments without rules, but the frequent superiority of them.

29. See Evelyn Waugh, *Robbery under Law* (Akadine Press, 1999), 17.

Chapter Seven

1. The fact that some favorites are freely chosen, rather than given, does not diminish the strength of one's commitment to them. In some cases, it seems to intensify one's commitment. Americans, living in a smorgasbord of options, often pick their own religious tribes. They may inherit a religion, but many also go beyond that inheritance and choose a spiritual path later in life. Once they fasten on their new choice (e.g., conversion or becoming born-again, etc.), they can become exceedingly dogmatic and fanatical about it.

2. That's because favoritism attachment is only partly conscious. It is also a chemical imperative that remains invisible to the conscious mind. Internet dating services are actually trying to use this invisible preference information to find good matches for searching singles. What people "say" they want in a partner and what they really want are not always the same (due to obvious social stigmas and also the less acknowledged but equally important fact that people are often dishonest with themselves about what they like). Add to this problem the new insight that passionate romantic love has a very different set of chemicals associated with it than long-term bonding. The "crush" or infatuation (otherwise known as the lightning bolt) is correlated with high levels of dopamine in the brain, and the "Honey, where's the remote?" and the "When are the grandchildren coming over?" long-termers have higher levels of oxytocin hormones.

Sometimes your chemicals are pushing you for immediate sexual gratification, and sometimes your chemicals are pushing you for long-term stability (for women it's the "bad boy versus nice guy" scenario, and for men it's the "femme fatale versus the house frau" scenario).

Now add to this the fact that your genome is trying to reproduce itself with the most "fit" mate possible, because that will ensure a better immune system in your kids. Sometimes it seems that this unconscious genetic agenda is actually playing us like puppets in the realm of romance. For example, Claus Wedekind of the University of Lausanne in Switzerland, performed an experiment on forty-nine women. He asked the women to sniff sweaty T-shirts that had been worn by unidentified men and to rank their stank from best to worst (I'm not making this up—see Lauren Slater, "Love," *National Geographic*, February 2006, 33–49). The test confirmed that women "preferred" the scent of men whose genotype was most different from their own—and diverse gene mixing is one proven way to make healthier babies. Unfortunately, the best baby-making partner (from the genetic point of view) is not always the best stable partner (from the child-rearing compatibility point of view). Sometimes the intense sparks between lovers produces a child that has a strong élan vital, but then ironically those same sparks make the subsequent child-rearing partnership very difficult.

3. See W. H. Auden, introduction to Henry James's *The American Scene*, in *The Complete Works of W. H. Auden Prose*, Vol. II (Princeton University Press, 2002). Thanks to Rami Gabriel for calling my attention to Auden's introduction.

4. As Richard Rorty says, "We need a redescription of liberalism as the hope that culture as a whole can be 'poeticized' rather than as the Enlightenment hope that it can be 'rationalized' or 'scientized.'" See Rorty, *Contingency, Irony and Solidarity* (Cambridge University Press, 1989), 53. To my mind, Rorty also gets suckered by the old false dichotomy of self versus group. He describes the modern Westerner as a compromise between the "strong poet" and the "repressed bureaucrat"—the romantic individual versus the state. But he also misses the middle way of fundamental tribal affiliation. The nepotistic tribal value system precedes Rorty's two categories, I would argue, and offers a real solution to the fractured, alienated value systems of modernity.

5. See Stefan Klein, *The Science of Happiness* (Marlowe & Co., 2006), for a summary of the neuroscientific bases of human happiness.

6. See Barry Schwartz, *The Paradox of Choice: Why More Is Less* (Harper Perennial, 2005).

7. Ibid., 110.

8. Rensis Likert, *The Human Organization: Its Management and Values* (McGraw-Hill, 1967), 64.

9. There are limits, of course, to these relaxations of standards, and people are pretty good at judging the limit of their own forbearance. If you're loyal to someone who consistently fails and never really fulfills expectations (e.g., a drug addict), then you can't sustain the relationship. Or if you are dutifully applying all loyalty possible to your spouse and then find him/her cheating on you, well, loyalty is not the same as stupidity.

10. Obviously, I'm trying to characterize genuine gratitude here and know full well that some characters are cynically grateful and would love to "get one over on you." But

cases of faux gratitude (and the ubiquity of free riders) don't negate the kind of virtue analysis I'm doing here.

11. The ethics of "care" needs to be mentioned here. One of the most compelling objections to the egalitarian version of ethics has come from feminism. From Mary Wollstonecraft (1759–1797) to Carol Gilligan (b. 1936), women have noticed that the *ideal* of utilitarianism and Enlightenment rule-based ethics has been the "autonomous man." But what about the "communal woman"? See Rosemarie Tong, *Feminine and Feminist Ethics* (Wadsworth, 1993), for a good contrast of the autonomous man and communal woman paradigms. Carol Gilligan's important work on care-based ethics arose out of her critique of masculine models of developmental moral psychology. See her *In a Different Voice: Psychological Theory and Women's Development* (Harvard University Press, 1982). Feminists noticed that the typical model of the Western ethical man was an utterly detached, impartial self. This autonomous self was supposed to have pulled himself out of the subjective quagmire of emotions and biased attachments, in order to view the objective fair distribution of goods with a disinterested eye. "Bollocks," said women philosophers, who knew full well that this "autonomous self" was a total fiction (or a twisted pathology). Moreover, women pointed out that social knowledge itself must be particular, not universal; concrete, not abstract; and emotionally valenced, not just mathematical.

Care is an alternative to principle-based fairness because it acknowledges the inextricable intimacies of human social life, and it places emotions at the root of those intimacies. But the intimacies of care also create special obligations and duties that constrain us and act as quasi-laws (more particular than universal, but still binding).

This is the kind of ethical framework that can acknowledge special cases, like Kongzi's sheep-stealing father or the Euthyphro case. And care-based ethics is poised to make a big comeback in light of increasing data from affective neuroscience about the chemistry of social bonding and the origins of our ethical values. The aspect of care-based ethics that still needs development is how to build a large-scale social justice standard from these perspectival roots. Carol Gilligan and Grant Wiggins address this in "The Origins of Morality in Early Childhood Relationships," in *Mapping the Moral Domain*, ed. Carol Gilligan, Janie Victoria Ward, and Jill McLean Taylor (Harvard University Press, 1988), but the full construction remains a promissory note. Psychologist Lawrence Kohlberg criticized Gilligan's care model on the grounds that it could not solve conflicting social justice claims—there was no relevant "moral point of view." Gilligan responded to Kohlberg, saying her morality of care "represents not merely the sphere of 'personal decision making,' as he puts it, but an alternative point of view from which to map the moral domain and reveal 'the laws of perspective' (in Piaget's phrase) which describe a relationally grounded view of morality" (138).

12. Marx argued, in his 1844 Paris Manuscripts, that such institutionalized labor "alienates" human beings from their own creative potential (i.e., such mindless work sucks the life out of us), and that it also estranges us from one another (because we inevitably begin to see each other as "tools"). Such labor also alienates us, Marx contends, from many of the products of our labor, because we don't personally use the products in some cases.

13. And, of course, all ethics aside, many other kinds of labor and craft skills also need mentors, but we have less and less of this personal education in our culture.

14. Vigen Guroian, *Tending the Heart of Virtue* (Oxford University Press, 2002), 104.

15. I am thankful to Dr. Barry Schwartz for his careful and critical reading of my arguments and for his many insightful suggestions. This quote is from a personal communication.

16. I am indebted to Barry Schwartz for reminding me of this wonderful line from Graham Greene, *The Ministry of Fear: An Entertainment* (Penguin Classics, 2005), 166.

17. See Freud, *Civilization and Its Discontents* (Norton, 2005), 63.

18. Kudos to my editor Elizabeth Branch Dyson for coming up with this hilarious social group.

19. David Levy, *Love and Sex with Robots* (Harper Perennial, 2007).

20. William Godwin, *Enquiry Concerning Political Justice and Its Influence on Morals and Happiness*, vol. 1, the Third Edition Corrected (Printed for G. G. and J. Robinson, Paternoster-Row, London, 1798).

INDEX

Page numbers followed by an *f* indicate figures.